Lord, Teach us to Pray

Twenty-one Days of Developing Spiritual Practices

Tony Whelan

Cover photo and design by Julie Palermo
(Julie.Palermo@hotmail.com)

ISBN-10: 1475092288
EAN-13: 9781475092288

"You are precious in my eyes;
you are honoured
and I love you."
Isaiah 43:4

Dedicated to my parents, who gave me the gifts of life and of faith.
To my daughters, Emily and Janet, as well as my students-
may the richness of the faith I inherited be yours.

Contents

Introduction

You are free. Before you begin this book I want to make clear that you are free to believe and to practice your faith in whatever way you choose. It's up to you. Faith and spirituality is very personal and must be freely chosen.

To be free is to be responsible for yourself. You are responsible not only for what you do, but also for who you become. Allow me to illustrate with a story:

An old Cherokee was teaching his grandson about life:

"A fight is going on inside me," he said to the boy. "It is a fight between two wolves. One is evil - pride, envy, greed, gluttony, lust, anger and laziness. The other is good - he is love, joy, peace, patience, kindness, goodness, gentleness, faithfulness and self-control. The same fight is going on inside you - and inside everyone."

The grandson thought about it for a minute and then asked his grandfather, "Which wolf will win?"

The old Cherokee simply replied, "The one you feed."

Choosing to pray and develop yourself spiritually is choosing to feed the good wolf. I am not saying you will be perfect. In fact it is the recognition that we are far from perfect that makes us want to work at it. I am saying that you will grow in virtue, in the qualities of *love, joy, peace, patience, kindness, goodness, gentleness, faithfulness, and self-control*. These qualities are known as the fruits of the Holy Spirit, listed in Galatians 5:22. These are the qualities of God. *"God is love"* (1 Jn. 4:8). They are called fruits of the Holy Spirit because they *grow* in a person under the influence of the Holy Spirit, a person under the influence of perfect love. These qualities will grow in a person who takes time for prayer.

Jesus calls us to know God's love deeply and let it show in our actions. He had great difficulty with those whose religiousness was only for show. *"Beware of false prophets, who come to you disguised as sheep but underneath are ravenous wolves. You will be able to tell them by their fruits"* (Mt. 7:15-16).

Why twenty-one days?

This book teaches twenty one ways of prayer. Why twenty-one? I recently heard the Franciscan priest and writer Richard Rohr say that it takes twenty-one days to form a new habit. I looked it up and found that this comment is actually based on the bestseller *Psycho-Cybernetics*, by Dr. Maxwell Maltz. He was originally a plastic surgeon, and he noticed that it took twenty-one days for amputees to cease feeling phantom sensations in the amputated limb. From further observations he found it took twenty-one days to create a new habit. Brain circuits take memory traces and produce neuroconnections and neural pathways only if they are bombarded for twenty-one days in a row. This means that the brain will only accept new data for a change of habit if the change is repeated each day for twenty-one days in a row.

This book has twenty-one chapters and I suggest you make time for a chapter a day. Each chapter will teach a different way of prayer, which you are invited to try. If you spend some time each day in prayer for twenty-one days in a row, daily prayer will become a habit. As you continue past twenty-one days, the habit will grow stronger still.

Perhaps you already have a habit of stopping for prayer each day, but if you don't, then beginning to do so could be life-changing. You will become more conscious of yourself as a spiritual being, and more conscious of God's loving presence and action in your life.

Aristotle wrote that we learn justice by practicing justice and we learn goodness by doing good. We learn to play the violin by practicing the violin. In the same way we learn to pray by praying.

In Robert Wicks's book, *Touching the Holy*, he writes, "Although taking fifteen or twenty minutes to be with God each day in silence and solitude sounds good (and easy in theory), the reality is obviously very different."[1] Wicks discusses some reasons why we tend to resist spending time in prayer and reflection and suggests we don't want to face our real selves. We don't trust enough in the goodness of God. Such honesty with a God who sees all is unnerving, and so "unconsciously knowing this leads many of us to develop a schedule in which we become too active to slow down and too full to make room for God."[2]

Do you feel that the topic of God and your spiritual life is worth pursuing? It seems obvious to me that most in our society really don't believe it is very important at all. People's priorities can be seen in how they spend their time and energy. The fact that you are reading this book suggests that you have an interest in spirituality.

If you don't feel that prayer is important, you probably won't pray. There are too many other things competing for your attention. As Fr. Hilary Ottensmeyer, a deceased monk of Saint Meinrad Archabbey said, "Until you are convinced that prayer is the best use of your time, you will not find the time for prayer."

Can prayer be taught?

"Now once he was in a certain place praying, and when he had finished one of his disciples said, 'Lord, teach us to pray.'" (Luke 11:1)

Richard Rohr had the following to say about the Church's call to teach prayer: "When the Church is no longer teaching the people how to pray, we could almost say it will have lost its reason for existence. Prayer is the ultimate empowerment of the people of God. Overemphasis on social prayer has left many of our people passive, without a personal prayer life and comfortable with 'handed-down religion' instead of first-hand experience."[3] That is what we are longing for: first-hand experience of God.

Recently I came out of a bakery with a free sample of cake in my hand. My wife saw me eating it and asked what it tasted like. I could have started to describe it: "It has a hint of cinnamon with some nutmeg…" I did not even try. I simply gave her a piece. Try it and see how it tastes. We could say the same of

---

1 Robert J. Wicks, *Touching the Holy*, (Notre Dame: Ave Maria Press, 1992), 40.

2 Ibid., 41.

3 Rohr, Richard, *Everything Belongs*, Crossroad Publishing, New York, 2003, p. 147.

God: *"Taste and see that the Lord is Good."* (Ps. 34:8) That is why I encourage you to learn ways of prayer – so you can taste and see the goodness of God.

That is what I hope for more than anything else for my children and for the students I serve: that they come to know first-hand the goodness of God. It's one thing for religion to give us moral guidance and rules, but quite another to experience inner transformation. Once you experience God within yourself and within others, respect and care for one another follows very naturally. It's no longer a matter of rules. St. Augustine said, "Love God and do as you will." If we know and love God we will *want* to pray and we will *want* to serve. Rules are important, but our virtue has to go *"deeper than that of the scribes and Pharisees."* (Matthew 5:20)

I came to experience God because of the grace of God and the witness and words of genuine ministers of the Gospel. This experience of a God who is unconditional love changed everything and from that time I began to commit myself to prayer, to learning about God and sharing what I had learned. But God cannot be explained or taught. God has to be *experienced.* Prayer can be taught, but it is only by the *practice* of prayer that we can come to experience God.

I hope you will try the twenty-one ways of prayer I introduce in this book. Some of these you may do already. Some may be new to you and you may want to try them - so that you can taste for yourself and see the goodness of God.

If you practice one a day over the next twenty one days, then in three weeks you will have developed a habit of stopping for prayer. At the very least, the act of stopping at the same time and same place each day will become a habit. You are also sure to grow in your spirituality, to grow in faith, hope and love.

During the twenty-one spiritual practices, I invite you to jot a few notes about your experience of each type of prayer. Then at the end of the three weeks you can review and decide which spiritual practices are best suited for you. Prayer is very personal, so it's up to you.

Five to ten minutes a day

You will only need about five to ten minutes a day to work through this book, although more time could be given to some prayer forms. It might help to make a plan. Where and when will you commit to spend time over the next twenty-one days so you can develop a habit of prayer? The end of the day, when everything else is done first, may not be the best time. Consider setting your alarm ten minutes earlier. Perhaps during your lunch break or after work.   Choose the time that would be best for you. Give God the best – not the rest.

If the practice of prayer is something new for you, then the book you hold in your hand could change your life. How can a mere five minutes a day change your life? It can because this time is the basis for forming a relationship with God and living it out the rest of your day and your life. Saint Paul says in his first letter to the Thessalonians, "*Pray at all times*" (5:17). That is the ultimate goal: that our whole day be lived as prayer, with a sense of God's presence and action. *The Catechism of the Catholic Church* says the following about these words of St. Paul: "But we cannot pray 'at all times' if we do not pray at specific times, consciously willing it" (Par 2697). That is why it is so important to put aside time for prayer.

The founder of L'Arche and a prophet of our time, Jean Vanier, has said that regular prayer is absolutely necessary: "Ladies and gentlemen, we must have a firm and steadfast resolution to give at least some few moments each day to prayer, to letting the eternal values penetrate our lives. And may I suggest that this prayer is not an added luxury in our lives, something spiritual to give greater insight, but an absolute necessity."[4] If we really believed this, we would make prayer a priority and find the time.

Three types of prayer

The *Catechism of the Catholic Church* defines three types of prayer: "The Christian tradition comprises three major expressions of the life of prayer: vocal prayer, meditation, and contemplative prayer." (par 2721) The first four days of prayer will introduce various vocal prayers, beginning with the Lord's Prayer. We will then move on to meditation. "Meditation is above all a quest. The mind seeks to understand the why and how of the Christian life." (par 2705) Various ways of meditating on life and meditating with scripture wil be introduced. Vocal prayer and meditation will overlap and can easily lead to contemplation at any time. Contemplation is simply resting in God's presence. "Contemplative prayer is the simplest expression of the mystery of prayer. It is a gift, a grace." (par 2713) The experience of God's presence is the most beautiful experience we can know. It is a gift we can do nothing to earn. Prayer is the way we open our hearts to receive this gift of God's grace.

---

4 Jean Vanier, *Jean Vanier, Essential Writings*, ed. Carolyn Whitney-Brown, (Toronto: Novalis, 2008), 154.

Experimentation

The idea of this book is to experiment with various types of prayer to see which ones work for you. Some will work for you and some won't.

We know that in baseball a batter is allowed two strikes and only has to connect once to be successful; and if he gets a hit forty percent of the time he steps up to the plate he is doing exceptionally well. Most of the time a batter steps up to the plate he won't get on base. Baseball is accepting of failure as part of the game.

Experimenting with anything new can be like that. If only a fraction of these prayers work for you, that's fine. The idea is to experiment to find out which ones do and which ones don't.

St. John of the Cross said that "To come to the knowledge you have not, you must go by a way in which you know not." In other words, in order to learn something new you have to be willing to try something new. If you experiment with an open mind, and you may be led to an experience you never could have imagined.

Self-Evaluation

So let's say you have decided prayer is something worth your time and you have decided you would like to give a few minutes each day for the next twenty-one days. You first need to assess the effort you are giving it now before you decide where to go from here. Do you feel you are spending enough time in prayer? Do you stop everything else on a regular basis so you can give all your attention to God, just as you would for someone you are truly in love with?

If there is need for improvement, can you name specifically what needs to be improved? Where should you start? Well, there is only one place to start, and that is right where you are. Begin before you are ready. God comes and meets us right where we are - never doubt that. And never say, "I am not good enough to come into God's presence." Of course you're not. None of us are. But that's the good news: God loves us just as we are. Again and again the self-righteous religious leaders of Jesus' time simply could not comprehend such a concept and were very threatened by it.

Gerald May (1940-2005), an MD well known for his writings on psychology and spirituality, wrote the following: "The prospect of really being loved no matter who we are, how we are, or what we do is so humbling that in spite of its reassurance it terrifies us. Thus we can remain frozen in the conviction that we must earn the experience of God through good behavior. Belief in this may be unwavering, in spite of the fact that every major religion – and most notably the Christian Gospel – proclaims just the opposite, that the experience of God is given, freely, to everyone and good behavior springs naturally from that experience when it is realized and accepted. This is the other option. But for many of us, it requires too much humility, too much surrender of self-importance."[5] This Gospel message of God's unconditional love has to not only be heard but "*realized and accepted*". This is what the spiritual journey is all about. The deep realization of this truth changes everything!

This good news of God's unconditional love should encourage us to be honest with ourselves. Take a few minutes to reflect. Do you have a habit of stopping for prayer each day? Are you satisfied with your prayer life? Would you like to improve your practice of the spiritual life? This book is intended to help you make that effort. A little bit of journaling might help. Write about your prayer life, your hopes, and most importantly *where and when* you will find five to ten minutes a day over the next twenty-one days.

"To fall in love with God is the greatest of all romances; to seek God, the greatest adventure; to find God, the greatest human achievement."

St. Augustine

---

5 Gerald May, *Will and Spirit*, (San Francisco, Harper, 1982), 140.

Day One

The Lord's Prayer

When the disciples asked Jesus, *"Lord, teach us to pray,"* this is the prayer Jesus taught. It is known as the Lord's Prayer.

> *Our Father, who art in heaven*
> *Hallowed be thy name.*
> *Thy kingdom come, thy will be done*
> *On earth as it is in heaven.*
> *Give us this day our daily bread.*
> *And forgive us our trespasses*
> *As we forgive those who trespass against us.*
> *And lead us not into temptation*
> *But deliver us from evil.*

Sometimes when a prayer becomes very familiar, we lose sight of its depth. There is much in this prayer that invites further reflection.

When Jesus introduced this prayer and said, *"You should pray like this."* (Matt. 6:9) He didn't say to use the exact words but simply to pray *"like this."* You may want to try praying the same ideas but in your own words.

For example, you begin with the idea of *"Our Father, who art in heaven, Hallowed be thy name."* You may want to address God with a different image from the one of Father. Father is one biblical image, but the scripture also refers to God as a mother: *"Like a son comforted by his mother will I comfort you"* (Isa. 66:13). Whether you prefer this mother image or the traditional father image is very personal. I prefer the biblical images of spirit, light and love (*"God is Spirit"* (John 4:24), *"God is Light"* (1 John 1:5), *"God is Love"* (1 John 4:8, 12) - so I might address God in this way: "O Great Spirit, God of light, God of love, holy is your name!" These thoughts of God's greatness fill me with awe. I stop with this thought and praise God's greatness. No matter which image or words you use, the important thing is to pause and enjoy how wonderful our glorious God is. Stay with it for a while with your arms raised if you want and praise God for being so incredibly awesome!

The next part of the prayer asks for God's reign to come in our lives (*"Thy kingdom come"*) and for God's will to be done, which is really one and the same thing. God is reigning, or exercising kingship, when his will is being done. If God is the spirit or pure energy of love and light, then we are praying for love and light to reign in our lives, to be the most important thing in our lives. Of course, God never forces his will. Praying this is an act of choosing to consent to God's reign in your heart. Again, we do well to pause with this thought and really pray it.

In the first letter of John, the Apostle wrote, "*We know that we belong to God, but the whole world lies in the power of the Evil One.*" Now the world is not evil, but the way things are run is evil. "Money makes the world go round" is a common saying that is all too true. The United Nations reported in February of 2012 that five children around the world die every minute because of chronic malnutrition! We like to think that God is in charge, but it should be very obvious when we look at the state of the world today that God is not in charge here. That is why we are instructed to pray that God's reign will come. In Paul's letter to the Romans he says that the kingdom of God "*means justice and peace and joy brought by the Holy Spirit*" (14:17). The kingdom of God is in people who choose to make the effort to allow justice, peace, and joy to reign in their hearts and in their lives.[6]

God's will in our lives, as Christians, is that we love and live like Jesus, which means sacrificing like Jesus, too. Extending our arms so that our body makes the sign of the cross is appropriate for this part of the prayer. We are saying with our body that we are willing to sacrifice ourselves in love as Jesus did on the cross. It is when we do this that God's kingdom is within us as it is in heaven. It is when we do this that we can become instruments of peace. Pause here and stay with the prayer for a while. You may even start to think of ways you are called to do God's will in a specific area of your life.

At different times in your life different words in the Lord's Prayer will stand out to you. There was a time when I would often pause on the words "*lead us.*" Those are two very important words worth dwelling on. Another person might pause on "*forgive us*" or "*as we forgive.*" That might be a good time to stop and reflect on whom you need to forgive. It is a good time to pray for your enemy and to ask for the grace to forgive. It is not natural to forgive your enemy, and that is why we pray for the grace.

You may incorporate other gestures as well, such as cupping your hands in front of you with the words, "*Give us this day our daily bread.*" I like to bless myself with the sign of the cross with each of the last three petitions, since it is by Jesus' cross that we are forgiven, find the grace to forgive, and are delivered from evil.

Don't be shy about using physical gestures to pray. It may be helpful to pray in private: "*When you pray, go to your private room and, when you have shut your door, pray to your Father.*" (Matt. 6:6)

---

6 An excellent book about Jesus, his mission, and vision of the Kingdom Of God was written by James Nolan, *Jesus Before Christianity.* (Orbis Books, 1976, 2001)

The gestures you use are up to you. It may even change from day to day. Some people love to kneel by the bed and pray. The important thing is that you spend some time *really* praying the ideas and feelings behind the words. Pray with your body and with all your heart.

If you ever feel like you don't know what to pray, the Lord's Prayer is one you can always fall back on. St. Thérèse of Lisieux, the nineteenth century Carmelite nun whose autobiography has sold millions, says the following of the Lord's Prayer: "Sometimes, when I'm in such a state of spiritual dryness that I can't find a single thought in my mind which will bring me close to God, I say an Our Father and a Hail Mary very slowly indeed. How they take me out of myself then; what solid satisfaction they give me." [7]

It is worth noting here that this great saint experienced "spiritual dryness". If it happened to her, we can expect that we will have times of dryness as well, when we cannot imagine or feel God. Mother Theresa experienced this for over fifty years. An important point is that the saints continued to pray and serve whether they *felt* God's presence or not. The Spirit of God is far beyond and much deeper than our thoughts and feelings.

For your first day in these twenty-one days of prayer, pray with these words Jesus taught, or perhaps use your own paraphrase of the words. Begin by lifting your arms and praising God with all your heart.

Notes:

_____

_____

_____

_____

_____

_____

_____

7 Thérèse of Lisieux, *Autobiography of Saint Thérèse of Lisieux*, trans. Ronald Knox, (New York: P.J. Kenedy & Sons, 1958), 290.

Day Two

St. Francis' Paraphrase of the Lord's Prayer

Some may think that since Jesus gave the words to the Lord's Prayer that it would be wrong to make any changes. Well, the saints did it. Following is the paraphrase of the Lord's Prayer written by St. Francis of Assisi in the thirteenth century. For this second day of prayer today, I invite you to read through his version. Take your time to meditate and pray with his words. Feel free at any time to add your own as well:

Our Father: Most Holy, our Creator and Redeemer, our Savior and our Comforter.

Who art in Heaven: in the angels and the saints. Who gives them light so that they may have knowledge, because Thou, Lord, are Light. Who inflames them so that they may love, because Thou, Lord, are Love. Who lives continually in them and who fills them so that they may be happy, because Thou, Lord, are the Supreme Good, the Eternal Good, and it is from Thee that all good comes, and without Thee there is no good.

Hallowed be Thy Name: May our knowledge of Thee become ever clearer, so that we may realize the extent of Thy benefits, the steadfastness of Thy promises, the sublimity of Thy Majesty and the depth of Thy judgments.

Thy Kingdom come: so that Thou may reign in us by Thy grace and bring us to Thy Kingdom, where we shall see Thee clearly, love Thee perfectly, be blessed in Thy company and enjoy Thee forever.

Thy will be done on earth as it is in Heaven: so that we may love Thee with our whole heart by always thinking of Thee; with our whole mind by directing our whole intention toward Thee and seeking Thy glory in everything; and with all our strength by spending all our powers and affections of soul and body in the service of Thy Love alone. And may we love our neighbors as ourselves, encouraging them all to love Thee as best we can, rejoicing at the good fortune of others, just as it were our own, and sympathizing with their misfortunes, while giving offense to no one.

Give us this day our daily bread: Thy own beloved Son, our Lord Jesus Christ, to remind us of the love He showed for us and to help us understand and appreciate it and everything that he did or said or suffered.

And forgive us our trespasses: in Thy infinite Mercy, and by the power of the Passion of Thy Son, our Lord Jesus Christ, together with the merits and the intercession of the Blessed Virgin Mary and all your saints.

As we forgive those who trespass against us: and if we do not forgive perfectly, Lord, make us forgive perfectly, so that we may indeed love our enemies for love of Thee, and pray fervently to Thee for them, returning no one evil for evil, anxious only to serve everybody in Thee.

And lead us not into temptation: hidden or obvious, sudden or unforeseen.

But deliver us from evil: Present, past, or to come.

Amen.[8]

Once you have read St. Francis's inspiring words, it may help to put down the book and raise your arms as you pray again the Lord's prayer in your own way, with your body and with all your heart.

Notes:

---

8 *This translation is based on that of Benen Fahy, OFM, as it appeared in The Writings of St. Francis of Assisi (London: Burnes & Oates, 1964).*

Day Three

The Glory Be

Glory to the Father,
and to the Son,
and to the Holy Spirit.
As it was in the beginning.
is now, and will be forever.

This prayer is very simple but contains so much. As with any prayer, it is important to really think about what you are praying. God is glorious and you are simply expressing your praise to God for his great glory. As with the previous two prayers, you would do well to raise your arms as you give glory to God. As you say "Glory to the Father," pause for a while and become conscious of the greatness of God, whom you are addressing, and do the same as you think of the other two persons of the trinity.

I find that a small change in the wording can make a big difference. Rather than saying "Glory to the Father," you might want to say "Glory to *you* Father," or "Glory to *you*, God of light, God of love!" Make it your own, and make it from the heart. Stay with each person of the trinity giving thanks and praise.

The second part of the prayer is also worth stopping to contemplate. Pause and think about time in the past. I like to change the words a bit here and say, "As it has been for all time." God is eternal, and to think of all time is really a mind-blowing thought.

Next you come to the present. Consciousness of the now and being fully present to the now, can be a liberating thought. God is always present in the moment – not in the past or the future. As you fully enter the moment, realize that *right now* is also part of eternity. Think about that. Your present moment right now is part of eternity. Hopefully our eternity will be spent praising the glory of God with all the saints and angels, and we are taking part in that even now. As we conclude with "and will be forever," we are again reminded that our God is an eternal God whom we are called to be with for all time!

In the Gospel of John, Jesus says, *This is eternal life: to know you, the only true God, and Jesus Christ whom you have sent.*" (John 17:3) When we experience and glorify God in prayer we are experiencing eternal life. That is no small thing!

It has been said that prayer is lifting our minds and hearts to God. That is what we are doing when we pray this prayer, if we pray from the heart and are mindful of what we are saying.

The beauty of this short prayer is that it can be prayed any time you feel like praising God. You could be out in nature and be inspired to praise, or in school or at work and have a few seconds to give glory to God.

Spend some time with it today. For this, your third day, pray this traditional prayer with all your mind and heart. Allow yourself to experience *now* as part of all time that has ever been and that will ever be; experience this moment as participating in eternity. God is in the present moment.

For this third day of prayer, you may want to combine the Lord's Prayer with the Glory Be. In this way your prayer will begin and end with praise to God.

Just as with physical exercise, repetition can be a good practice for prayer as well. You may want to repeat the Our Father and Glory Be five or even ten times. You may find that with more repetitions you move deeper and deeper into the spirit of the words. I like to repeat these prayers as I hold a set of beads in my hand that has fifteen beads so I finish when I get to the end of the beads. At the same time, don't make the mistake of thinking that the more you pray, the more your prayer will be heard. It is better to pray one word from your heart than to pray a thousand words only from your lips.

Notes:

_____

_____

_____

_____

_____

_____

_____

_____

Day Four

Wisdom Literature/Spiritual Reading

There are many great books that can help us learn about and live the spiritual life. Some favorite spiritual writers of mine are Richard Rohr, Ronald Rolheiser, and Henri Nouwen. Joyce Rupp is the best I know for writing prayers that can be used for any occasion.

Sometimes the writing of someone you know and love can be especially inspiring. For today's prayer, I invite you to reflectively read the following piece from my mother's autobiography, which she gave to each of her children before she passed away. First let me explain what the writing is about.

At the age of nineteen, while in training for the religious life a thousand miles from home, I received a phone call from my father that I will never forget. My father told me that Janet, my eighteen-year-old sister, had drowned. My father, two brothers and another sister were on the rocks at Cape Spear, the most easterly point in North America, when she was hit by a rogue wave and swept out to sea.

That May evening as I tried to sleep, a young bird chirped incessantly through the night. It was still the Easter season and I think an Easter egg lay freshly opened in a nest just outside my window. It's funny how God gives little signs at times.

Here is the story told by my mother of another little sign that has become a part of our family's story. It begins about a month before Janet's death in 1980:

On weekends, it was common for Janet to work the closing shift, so coming home late was the norm and accepted, especially since she had the habit of coming to my bedside, kissing me and whispering good night.

One particular Friday night in April she was later than usual. I lay in bed in a state of semi-sleep when finally she crept in. We both glanced at the digital clock and I was about to admonish her for being late when she said, "Mom, it's only..." and then a pause, "4:44." I put my finger to my lips in a gesture of silence. We both knew it would be best not to waken her dad at that time.

The next day, a few of us were sitting around our kitchen table, and I checked to see if it was time to start supper. The clock was just turning over 4:44. Remembering the night before, I asked Janet to look at the time. She blushed, and I sensed her fear that I might tell her siblings about her late, late night. To spare her being teased, I just laughed and so did she. The others wanted to know what was so funny. I seized this moment to make this a "special secret" with Janet. We continued this ritual whenever we saw the numbers 444, and the more the others probed as to what it was all about, the more we enjoyed keeping them wondering.

On May 7, my sons Kevin and Chris came to St. John's for a visit. My two daughters Paula and Janet had just finished their winter semester and were free to spend a few days holidaying with their brothers. We celebrated Mother's Day that weekend. Our closest friends, Joe and Irene and their children, joined us for dinner. We sang songs and played cards. I was very happy and thankful to have five of our seven children with me for this special day.

The sun was shining brilliantly on Monday, May 12. It was an ideal day to visit Cape Spear National Park. Kevin took the day off work, and after lunch he, Paula, Janet, Kevin and Chris set out for an afternoon of fun and sightseeing. I thought it best to stay at home to be there for our son Michael when he came home from high school and to prepare chicken and home fries for dinner.

At approximately six o'clock I saw the car pull into the driveway, so I immediately dropped the cut potatoes into the deep fryer. I knew they all would be hungry and looking forward to one of their favorite meals. When I turned toward the door to greet them, my husband Kevin stood there in obvious pain. He reached out to take me in his arms and asked me to sit down because he had something sad to tell me. He said there had been a terrible accident while they were at Cape Spear, resulting in Janet's death. She had been hit by a huge, unexpected wave and swept out into the sea. His words shot through my heart like a knife. I shouted, "Jesus, help us!" Calmly and confidently he responded, "He will." My next words to Kevin were along the lines of, "Are you sure she is dead? Where is she? I've got to see her." He agreed to take me to the Health Sciences Centre…

That night I lay awake in bed, in a state of shock and confusion, wishing and praying that Janet could come home and whisper good night to me. I fell asleep for a brief time, only to wake up suddenly and see her right next to me, her face bearing a radiance of happiness. I reasoned this had to be a dream; yet the experience was so powerful that my heart knew otherwise. My bedside clock showed 4:44 a.m. I immediately remembered our secret. All traces of tiredness and sleep left me. Her presence stayed with me as I walked the few steps to her bedroom.

As I sat in her room I felt comforted and peaceful. I thought about our good times together, of the blessing she had been in my life. I rested for a couple of hours, then prepared for what I anticipated to be a rough day.

The numbers 444 kept showing up. I hesitated to tell anyone except Kevin about this, fearful that I would be looked upon as being fanatical or a weirdo. Finally, I spoke with Father Jim Davis, a priest friend whom I could trust. He suggested that each time I saw those triple digits to remember Janet in prayer. Eventually I felt comfortable enough to talk about it to our children and a few close friends. Some of them began noticing as well. We followed Fr. Jim's suggestion. This was one way of remembering Janet and staying connected. The practice has snowballed and over the years we have shared many stories and experiences around "444."[9]

I find this writing incredibly powerful. Here is what I have learned from Janet's death and my mother's writing.

First of all, God works in mysterious ways. In the gospels there are many resurrection appearances that happen in various ways. In the Gospel of Mark Jesus first appears to Mary of Magdala and then it says that *"He showed himself under another form to two of them as they were on their way into the country.* (v. 12) I

---

9   Regina Whelan, *Sketches of My Life*, (2004).

find it intriguing when the gospel says that he appeared *"under another form."* The point is that God reveals himself in various ways to different people, and each experience is unique. St. Thérèse of Lisieux encourages us to trust that God lovingly gives each of us the grace we need. She compares God's communication and gentle touch to sunlight: "The sun's light that plays on the cedar trees, plays on each tiny flower as if it were the only one in existence; and in the same way our Lord takes interest in each soul, as if it were the only one in existence." [10]

The second message is that life is short. We have to be able to accept death as a reality and a natural part of life, and our faith is a tremendous help. The realization of everlasting life gives a whole new perspective to everything. To see yourself as a spiritual being with an eternal destiny is a quantum leap from seeing yourself as just someone who lives for a time and that's it.

"I believe in the communion of saints... the resurrection of the body, and life everlasting," to quote the Apostles Creed. [11] To believe in the communion of saints is to believe that those who have died are still with us, in communion with us. They can communicate with us and us with them. We are all connected now and forever.

10 Lisieux, Autobiography, 35.

11 As for the mystery of what such a body might be like, see 1 Cor. 15:35-44. Also, Mark 12:18-27: *"When they rise from the dead... they are like the angels in heaven."* (v.25)

We have an eternal destiny, and to forget our spiritual and eternal life is very short sighted. We do well to note also that this eternity *includes now*.

Psalm 90 equates wisdom of the heart with knowing that life is short: "*Teach us to count how few days we have, and so gain wisdom of heart.*" (v. 12) The scriptures repeatedly remind us about the shortness of life: "*You are no more than a mist that is here for a little while and then disappears.*" (James 4:14) "*A person's life is but a puff of wind, our days are like a passing shadow.*" (Psalm 144:4)

Notes:

_____

_____

_____

_____

_____

_____

_____

_____

_____

Day Five

Mental Prayer

Many people lie in bed at night and just think about life, which often leads to thoughts of God. This may lead to talking to God about whatever is on the person's mind, or perhaps even wondering without words. This in itself is prayer.

Chapter two of Luke is about the birth of Jesus. Many wondrous things happened to Mary leading up to the birth, and it isn't surprising that she had much to ponder. At one point the Gospel says that Mary *treasured all these things and pondered them in her heart.*"(Luke 2:19) What a wonderful word: she *pondered* these events *in her heart.* That is mental prayer, a simple pondering with the heart.

St. Thérèse of Lisieux writes in her autobiography of her experience of mental prayer as a child: "One day, one of the mistresses at the Abbey asked what I did with myself on holidays, when I was left to my own devices. I told her that I got behind my bed, where there was an empty space in which you could shut yourself away with the curtains, and there... well, I used to think. 'Think about what?' she asked. 'Oh.' I said,' about God, and about life, and eternity; you know, I just think.' The dear nun made a great joke of this, and later on she used to remind me of my thinking days, and ask me whether I still thought. I can now see that I was practicing mental prayer without realizing what I was doing; God was teaching me the art in some secret way of his own." [12]

St. Thérèse says that God was teaching her the art of prayer. That is very significant. God can teach us prayer! In the Gospel of John, Jesus quotes the prophet Isaiah, saying, *"They will all be taught by God"* (6:45). In the first letter of St. John, he says, *"You do not need anyone to teach you; the anointing he gave you teaches you everything"* (2:27). This is an important concept. God teaches us to pray. That is why I chose the title for this book, *Lord, Teach us to Pray* (Luke 11:1). Ultimately, it is God who will teach you to pray as you spend time in prayer.

For this fourth day I invite you now to take five minutes to try this way of prayer. Close your eyes and wait. See what comes to mind. Let the ideas flow freely. Trust that the Spirit of God is at work in this. Think "about God, and about life, and eternity." Who is God for you? What is God like? You may talk to God in whatever way feels natural to you, or conclude with the Lord's Prayer and a Glory Be. You may even want to combine your pondering with writing in a journal or a walk in nature.

Notes:

_____

_____

_____

_____

_____

_____

_____

_____

_____

---

12   Lisieux, *Autobiography*, 101-102.

Day Six

Awareness Examen

"Unawareness is the root of all evil." - *Anonymous Egyptian monk*

For this type of prayer you need to put aside five to ten minutes. Close your eyes (Sometimes you need to close your eyes to see) and pray the prayer of the blind man in the Gospel: *"Lord, that I might see."* We pray here that the Holy Spirit will enlighten us to see his presence and action this day. Then you close your eyes and look over your day. If you are praying in the morning you can reflect on the previous day, or if you are praying in the evening, reflect on the day that has just passed. For some people nothing will come to mind at first. The key is to relax and *wait* to see what comes to mind.

When I close my eyes and look over my day, all kinds of incidents will begin to come to mind. The memories are there, just below the surface, if we just close our eyes and reflect. Pay attention to the significance of the memories. Listen to what God is saying to you in the events of your day. You may feel inspired to pray "thank you", or "sorry", or perhaps to place some concern in

God's hands. The important thing is that you look at the events of the day with God, and then pray as appropriate.

The Our Father prayed slowly and attentively is a good way to close the prayer time.

This is a great way to pray with others as well. Say a little prayer to the Holy Spirit and take time to reflect; after a minute or two, share what stood out for you from your day and close with an Our Father. What a great way for couples to pray, or a family.

Eckhart Tolle wrote an amazing book called *A New Earth*[13] in which he talks about the ego as the unobserved mind. The ego comprises the thoughts and feelings going on inside of us, and it is only ego when we mistakenly believe those thoughts and feelings are who we are. If we make a habit of taking an objective look at our thoughts and feelings, then we will not be controlled by our ego. As Richard Rohr wrote, "The ego self is the unobserved self. If you do not find an objective standing point from which to look back at yourself, you will almost always be egocentric – identified with yourself instead of in relationship to yourself."[14] To practice the awareness examen is to "find an objective standing point from which to look back at yourself."

Albert Einstein claimed, "Small is the number of them that see with their own eyes and feel with their own hearts." That is a very challenging point. Most of us are influenced in ways we do not even know. Advertisers, for instance, spend billions on advertising because they know it works. How influenced are we by our culture's "live to win" attitude rather than the Gospel's message, "live to give"? And how often do we go along with someone else just to fit in? This is not a new phenomenon. In John's Gospel, Jesus admonishes his listeners for worrying too much about what others think: *"How can you believe, since you look to one another for approval and are not concerned with the approval that comes from the one God?"* (John 5:44)

My daughter was recently asked to do an art assignment where she had to change something in our public environment to send a message. She decided to help people reflect by gluing mirrors along the top of the inside of a garbage can. The idea is that as people throw garbage in the can they will see themselves. Painted on the outside of the garbage is the message, "FACE YOUR GARBAGE." We all have sin and pain we would do well to deal with honestly rather than deny.

---

13 Plume Publications, New York, 2005.

14 Richard Rohr, *The Naked Now, Learning to See as the Mystics See*, (New York: Crossroad Publishing Co, 2009) 166.

Many in today's Western society live a shallow life, which leaves people unfulfilled; but it is probably even more dangerous to live in delusion. If we are motivated by repressed energies and motives which we are not even aware of, we are not free. It is important to be aware of why we do the things we do.

A grade twelve student named Suja James wrote the following reflection which demonstrates the importance of regular reflection: "Recently, every day I find myself questioning my purpose behind every action. What is the intention behind my action? Is it for my own benefit or truly and whole-heartedly am I doing it for others? Many months ago, I never bothered asking myself and eventually what I did was for my own benefit. Even today I am tempted to do everything for my own benefit. However, I have made the decision to pray and ask God to help me in loving and caring for others, even if it is just in giving them some of my time. It is difficult, but not impossible. Being human, I need my Lord to help me love others. Taking that moment to stop, reflect and pray, makes all the difference. Eventually, when our love is real, when it comes from the power of God's spirit, the Lord blesses you with the inner satisfaction that nothing else can give you." This writing demonstrates an uncommon attitude of humility and prayerfulness. Regular practice of the Awareness Examen leads us to be people who can be led and influenced by God.

Take a few moments now to reflect on your day. What arises for you to pray about? You may want to finish with the Our Father and/or the Glory Be.

Notes:

_____

_____

_____

_____

_____

_____

_____

_____

Day Seven

Prayer of Petition

"There is no need to worry; but if there is anything you need, pray for it" (Phil. 4:6).

I was once teaching a class of adults and asked if they spent time in prayer. One person from Ethiopia shared that he used to pray every day for his brother to return safely from war. When his brother never returned, he said he stopped praying and hadn't prayed since.

Sometimes our prayers are not answered as we wish, and sometimes they are. My father tells a story of being very sick with stomach troubles when he was newly married. He was bedridden for days. A priest came to visit, and while he was there the priest offered to bless his stomach. My father says that, with this offer from a priest the expectation in his mind was automatic; he expected that he would be healed and he was. It was as simple as that.

Prayer does not have to be so complicated. We should put aside time for prayer and we would do well to develop a pattern or habit of how we pray. But there will be times of spontaneous prayer as well. Once I was on a retreat being led by Sister José Hobday, a wonderful Native American sister who traveled extensively, leading retreats. She was quite elderly and couldn't see the clock, so she asked what time it was. In response she was given the time, "nine-eleven." Some chuckled at the coincidence, but she very seriously mentioned that the pope would be visiting ground zero tomorrow and stopped right there to voice a prayer for those who perished in the tragedy that was 9/11.

There will be times when we have an urgent need, and the scripture teaches us to pray for what we need, like a child asking parents for something. The great spiritual writer Anthony de Mello (1931-1987) wrote that many times he has met priests who prayed much better before they entered the seminary for their training. Why did they pray better before? Because it got too complicated. We used to pray for grace to pass our examinations, for health, for success in our work. "Then we grew up and learned a lot of clever arguments about God not being interested in these mundane trifles. God helps those who help themselves, we cannot change the will of God, etc. So we stopped expecting miracles; we stopped praying for miracles; and God's interventions in our lives became fewer and fewer." [15]

"St. John of the Cross says that people receive from God as much as they expect from God. If you expect little, you will generally receive little. If you expect much, you will receive much. Do you need a miracle of grace in your life? Then you must expect a miracle to happen."[16]

Of course we have all prayed for something and not received it. All prayers are answered, but sometimes the answer is no. St. Paul had a prayer request denied. He had something that was bothering him. We are not quite sure what it was. He referred to it as his *"thorn in the flesh."* It may have been a physical or mental ailment, or perhaps a person that was bothering him. Whatever it was, he wrote, *"About this thing I have pleaded with the Lord three times for it to leave me, but he has said, 'My grace is enough for you; my power is at its best in weakness"* (2 Cor. 12:8-9).

Even Jesus, before his death, prayed that he might not have to suffer: *"Abba (Father)! Everything is possible for you. Take this cup away from me. But let it be as you, not I, would have it."* (Mark 14:36) That last line is essential. As disciples of Jesus, we can expect that we may have to accept suffering at times, just as Jesus did. We are children of God, but we can't act like spoiled children who always have to have their own way. "In God's will is our peace."

---

15 Anthony deMello, *Contact with God*, (New York: Doubleday, 2003) 49.

16 *Ibid., p. 63.*

When Jesus promised, *"If you ask for anything in my name, I will do it."* (John 14:14) the *"in my name"* part is crucial. It's not that a prayer in Jesus's name is a magic formula, but that it is a prayer inspired by Jesus. It is a prayer Jesus would pray – in fact, He is praying in you. *"For when we cannot choose words in order to pray properly, the Spirit himself expresses our plea in a way that could never be put into words… The pleas of the saints expressed by the Spirit are according to the mind of God."* (Rom. 8:26-27)

Here is a true story about Corrie Ten Boom that illustrates well this principle of praying for something we know God would want: "Corrie and her family were imprisoned by the Nazis during World War II for hiding Jews in Amsterdam. Only Corrie survived. When the war ended, Corrie traveled about Europe, lecturing on forgiveness and reconciliation. After a talk in Munich, Germany, a man came up to thank her for the talk. He was one of the hated prison guards. When the man reached out to shake her hand, Corrie froze. She couldn't believe her response. She had just given a talk on forgiveness, and now she herself couldn't forgive the man. Corrie began to pray, saying, 'Jesus, I cannot forgive this man. Help me forgive him.' At that moment some mysterious power helped her reach out and take the man's hand in true forgiveness."[17]

St. James says, *"Why you don't have what you want is because you don't pray for it; when you do pray and don't get it, it is because you have not prayed properly; you have prayed for something to indulge your own desires"* (James 4:2-3). We have to be careful what we pray for. In the Lord's Prayer Jesus taught us to pray for *"our daily bread"* and *"Your kingdom come, your will be done, on earth as in heaven."* (Matthew 6:10-11) St. John puts it very nicely in his first letter: *"We are quite confident that if we ask him for anything, and it is in accordance with his will, he will hear us"* (1 John 5:14).

Following is a prayer by Henri Viscardi that demonstrates a lot of wisdom on this issue:

I asked God for strength that I might achieve. I was made weak that I might learn humbly to obey.

I asked God for health that I might do greater things. I was given infirmity that I might do better things.

I asked for riches that I might be happy. I was given poverty that I might be wise.

I asked for power that I might have the praise of men. I was given weakness that I might feel the need of God.

---

17 Mark Link, S.J., *Decision*, (Valencia: Tabor Publishing, 1988) 106.

I asked for all things that I might enjoy life. I was given life that I might enjoy all things.
I got nothing I asked for, but everything I had hoped for.
Almost despite myself, my unspoken prayers were answered. I am among all men most richly blessed.

What grace or gift of God's Spirit do you need to ask of God at this time? What would God want you to pray for? Reflect on this question and then ask in faith.

Notes:

_____

_____

_____

_____

_____

_____

_____

_____

_____

Day Eight

The Magnificat

"Mary said ... 'From this day forward all generations will call me blessed'" (Luke 1:48).

The Magnificat is one of my favorite prayers. This is the prayer of praise that Mary offered in her joy soon after being told by the angel Gabriel that she was to be the mother of the long awaited messiah. It is found in chapter one of the Gospel of Luke. The founder of L'Arche, Jean Vanier, refers to this as Mary's little gospel, because it sums up the good news of the Gospel message.

My soul proclaims the greatness of the Lord,
My Spirit rejoices in God my Saviour
For He has looked with favour on His lowly servant.
From this day all generations will call me blessed:
The Almighty has done great things for me,
And holy is His Name.
He has mercy on those who fear Him
In every generation.

He has shown the strength of His arm,
He has scattered the proud in their conceit.
He has cast down the mighty from their thrones,
And has lifted up the lowly.
He has filled the hungry with good things,
And the rich He has sent away empty.
He has come to the help of His servant Israel
For He has remembered His promise of mercy,
The promise He made to our fathers,
To Abraham and his children for ever.

This is essentially a prayer of praise and thanks for all the amazing things God has done. You may want to recall God's blessings toward you before you begin. I find it helpful to pray before an icon of Mary and various saints, along with pictures of family alive and deceased. It inspires me to be extremely thankful and to remember that we do not live only for this life. You may find that arranging such a prayer space could help in your prayer.

The prayer begins with *"My soul proclaims the greatness of the Lord."* St. Bonaventure said that the soul has three faculties: memory, intellect, and will. So if you use your memory to recall God's goodness to you, you are using your soul. If your intellect understands that God is your creator who has blessed you with life, again you are starting this prayer with your soul. Your will is the most important part of your soul, for that is the faculty that chooses to praise and serve God.

Each person who prays this will be praising and thanking God for different things. Each one of us has our own struggles and stories of blessings.

As with the Lord's Prayer, you may want to pray with your body. You begin with arms raised as you *"Proclaim the greatness of the Lord."* You may be moved to bow low, maybe at the line, *"He has mercy on those who fear Him"* and then rise up again with *"and has lifted up the lowly."*

Priests and those in religious communities in the Catholic Church pray this every day as part of their evening prayer. I recommend that you make it part of your daily prayer routine as well. Try reflecting on the great blessings in your life and praising God with this prayer. It is customary to finish this prayer with the Glory Be.

I like to pray the Magnificat, ending with the Glory be and then the Lord's Prayer. Try it; it's a great combination because they all involve praise and glory to God.

Notes:

_____

_____

_____

_____

_____

_____

_____

_____

_____

Rosary beads would be helpful for the next two days of prayer.

Day Nine

The Rosary

I remember when I was a teenager and I first came to consciously believe that there really is a God. I said to myself, "I guess I should pray." I was not in the habit and didn't have a clue where to begin. Then at church I came across a pamphlet about the rosary. I took it home, found rosary beads, knelt by my bed, and proceeded to follow the pamphlet closely. It was a long haul, as I prayed the Hail Mary one hundred and fifty times, along with all the other prayers. Only later did I learn that people usually pray five decades of the rosary a day rather than all fifteen! I was relieved to learn this and had a good chuckle at my own expense.

In praying the rosary, it is helpful to hold the rosary beads in your hand, as there is a set prayer to say for each bead. The beads help you to keep track. As you hold the crucifix, you make the sign of the cross and pray the Apostles' Creed, which is a summary of the faith from the early church:

I believe in God, the Father almighty, creator of heaven and earth. I believe in Jesus Christ, his only Son, our Lord. He was conceived by the power of the

Holy Spirit and born of the Virgin Mary. He suffered under Pontius Pilate, was crucified, died and was buried. He descended into hell. On the third day he rose again. He ascended into heaven, and is seated at the right hand of the Father. He will come again to judge the living and the dead. I believe in the Holy Spirit, the Holy Catholic Church, the communion of saints, the forgiveness of sins, the resurrection of the body, and life everlasting. Amen.

On the first bead we pray an Our Father, then on the next three we pray three Hail Mary's for an increase in faith, hope, and love. The words of the Hail Mary are very scriptural:

Hail Mary, full of grace, the Lord is with thee (from Luke 1:28)
Blessed art thou amongst women, and blessed is the fruit of your womb, Jesus (from Luke 1:42)
Holy Mary, Mother of God,
Pray for us sinners now and at the hour of our death. Amen.

On the next bead you pray the Glory Be:

Glory be to the Father, the Son, and the Holy Spirit, Amen.

Then you pray five decades of the rosary. For each decade you pray an Our Father on the first, slightly separate bead, ten Hail Mary's on the ten beads, and then the Glory Be. As you pray the ten Hail Mary's, fingering the beads, along with the built-in repetition, helps you to focus your mind. As you repeat the ten Hail Mary's, think about the particular mystery from the life of Christ that you are meditating on. You might start with a small scripture reading about the event from the life of Christ, or you might use a pamphlet that has a scripture verse and a picture to help you see the scene in your mind. We usually pray the mysteries in this order:

Monday and Saturday – the Joyful Mysteries:
1. The Annunciation (Luke 1:26-38)
2. The Visitation (Luke 1:39-45)
3. The Birth of Jesus (Luke 2:1-20)
4. The Presentation of Jesus (Luke 2:22-32)
5. The Finding of Jesus in the Temple (Luke 2:41-50)

Tuesday and Friday – the Sorrowful Mysteries:
1. The Agony in the Garden (Luke 22:39-46)
2. The Scourging (John 19:1)
3. Jesus is Crowned with Thorns (Mark 15:17)
4. Jesus Carries his Cross (John 19:17)
5. Jesus Dies on the Cross (John 19:26-27)

Wednesday and Sunday – the Glorious Mysteries:
1. Jesus Rises from the Dead (John 20:19)
2. Jesus Ascends into Heaven (Mark 16:19)
3. The Holy Spirit Comes on the Apostles (Acts 2:1-13)
4. Mary Is Assumed into Heaven (see 2 Timothy 2:12)
5. Mary Is Crowned Queen of Heaven (Revelation 13;5-6)

Thursday – the Mysteries of Light (added by John Paul II in 2002):
1. Jesus's Baptism (Matthew 3:13-17)
2. The Wedding at Cana (John 2:1-12)
3. The Proclamation of the Kingdom of God (Mark 1:15)
4. The Transfiguration (Luke 9:28-36)
5. The Institution of the Eucharist (Luke 22:19-20)

The rosary is not for everybody. St. Thérèse of Lisieux struggled with it herself: "It's a terrible thing to admit, but saying the rosary takes it out of me more than any hair-shirt would; I do it so badly! Try as I will to put force on myself, I can't meditate on the mysteries of the rosary; I just can't fix my mind on them. For a long time I was in despair about it, this want of devotion. I couldn't understand it, because I have such a love for the Blessed Virgin that there ought to be no difficulty about saying prayers in her honor; her own favorite prayers too! Now I don't distress myself so much; it seems to me that the queen of heaven, being my Mother, must be aware of my good intentions, and that's enough for her."[18] This is a perfect example of the rule, "Pray as you can; don't pray as you can't."

To pray five mysteries of the rosary takes about fifteen minutes. If you don't have time for that, you might choose one or two to pray. You may want to choose two that suit your mood right now or the liturgical season of the Church. (Joyful mysteries at Christmas, Sorrowful in Lent, and Glorious at Easter) You

---

18 Lisieux, *Autobiography*, 289-290

may want to pray two mysteries that get to the heart of our faith: the death and resurrection of Jesus. If you don't have rosary beads, you can count the ten Hail Mary's on your fingers.

Notes:

_____

_____

_____

_____

_____

_____

_____

_____

Day Ten

The Chaplet of Divine Mercy

A chaplet is another prayer that can be said on the rosary beads, and there are various kinds of chaplets, often devoted to various saints or images of Jesus. The chaplet of divine mercy comes to the Church from Sister Faustina, a Polish mystic who lived in the early 1900's and was canonized by Pope John Paul II in 2000. A powerful quote from her says that "If you were to take *all* the sins that have *ever* been committed, they would only be a drop in the sea of God's love." Here is the method of praying the chaplet of divine mercy:

1. Begin with the Sign of the Cross, and on the first four beads pray one Our Father, one Hail Mary and the Apostles Creed.
2. Then on the Our Father beads (the ones between the sets of ten) say the following: Eternal Father, I offer You the Body and Blood, Soul and Divinity of Your dearly beloved Son, Our Lord Jesus Christ, in atonement for our sins and those of the whole world.
3. On the ten Hail Mary beads say the following each time: ***For the sake of His sorrowful passion, have mercy on us and on the whole world.*** (Repeat steps 2 and 3 for all five decades).

4. Conclude with three repetitions of the following prayer: Holy God, Holy Mighty One, Holy Immortal One, have mercy on us and on the whole world.

I have only recently discovered this prayer and have found that repeating these words of mercy has the effect of filling the mind and heart with a heightened awareness of Jesus's spirit of mercy. A person who prays this is sure to become a more compassionate person.

The prayer is addressed to God the Father and refers to Jesus' "sorrowful passion." When it says, "For the sake of his sorrowful passion" I like to imagine the risen Jesus who still carries the wounds of his crucifixion and pray to *Him*. You may choose to address the prayer to Jesus: "For the sake of *your* sorrowful passion..."

If you are without these words and want to pray it, don't worry about memorizing everything exactly. Just make it your own. The main part is to use your rosary beads to count five sets of ten: "For the sake of His sorrowful passion, have mercy on us and on the whole world." My own adaptation of this prayer is to pray the Lord's Prayer before each set of ten and the Glory Be at the end, as we do with the rosary.

Grab those rosary beads (or fingers) and give it a try.

Notes:

_____

_____

_____

_____

_____

_____

_____

_____

Day Eleven

The Angelus

The Angelus is a Catholic Marian prayer, traditionally prayed at noon. This prayer is really a celebration of Mary's perfect response when the angel Gabriel appeared to announce that she was to be the mother of God. The prayer at the end is essentially a prayer for the Holy Spirit (grace) to come into our hearts. We remember that God became what we are so that by God's grace we can become what God is.

If said by a group of people, the leader says the first part and the group responds with the second part (after the colon), but it can be prayed alone as well.

The Angel of the Lord declared to Mary: And she conceived of the Holy Spirit.

Hail Mary, full of grace, the Lord is with thee; blessed art thou among women and blessed is the fruit of thy womb, Jesus. Holy Mary, Mother of God, pray for us sinners, now and at the hour of our death. Amen.

Behold the handmaid of the Lord: Be it done unto me according to Thy word.

Hail Mary . . .

And the Word was made Flesh: And dwelt among us.

Hail Mary . . .

Pray for us, O Holy Mother of God: That we may be made worthy of the promises of Christ. Let us pray:

Pour forth, we beseech Thee, O Lord, Thy grace into our hearts; that we, to whom the incarnation of Christ, Thy Son, was made known by the message of an angel, may by His passion and cross be brought to the glory of His resurrection, through the same Christ Our Lord. Amen.

This prayer at the end is one of my favorite prayers because it covers three very important Christian events.   First of all, the incarnation, the event of God becoming flesh through Mary, "made known by the message of an angel." This is the event we celebrate at Christmas. The prayer also reminds us of Jesus' passion, death and resurrection, the event we celebrate at Easter. What was the next big event after Jesus' birth, death and resurrection? The coming of the Holy Spirit that we read about in Acts 2:1-12. This prayer is essentially asking God to "pour forth" his Grace, or Holy Spirit, into our hearts.

I personally don't say the Angelus every day, but I do use its closing prayer as the closing when I pray the chaplet of divine mercy. I pray for the Holy Spirit to bless my family and students. A prayer for the Holy Spirit is a request God will surely grant: *"If you who are evil know how to give your children what is good, how much more will the Father give the Holy Spirit to those who ask him?"* (Luke 11:13)

Give it a try.

Notes:

_____

_____

_____

_____

_____

_____

_____

_____

Day Twelve

Novena

A novena is when you say a prayer for nine days in a row, often asking a saint to pray for you. The name comes from the Latin *novem*, which means nine. The practice comes from the belief that the disciples prayed for nine days after Jesus's resurrection as they waited for the promised Holy Spirit. The first chapter of the book of Acts tells the story. Jesus says, *"You will receive power when the Holy Spirit comes on you, and then you will be my witnesses... As he said this he was lifted up while they looked on, and a cloud took him from their sight... They joined in continuous prayer, together with several women, including Mary the mother of Jesus."* (Acts 1: 8-14) Nine days later was the birth of the church with the event of Pentecost.

There are many types of novenas. Often people will pray a novena to a certain saint, using prayer cards which give you the words to say. One example is Sister Faustina's novena to divine mercy. She asked that a novena would be prayed for nine days before the feast of Divine Mercy, the second Sunday of Easter.

My daughter was being confirmed some years ago, and we made up our own novena. Each day at supper for the nine days before her confirmation, we said a prayer for one of the fruits of the Holy Spirit (since there happens to be nine:

love, joy, peace, patience, kindness, goodness, trustfulness, gentleness and self-control. (Gal. 5:22). Each day we wrote the word of the day on a wooden cross, which she kept as a remembrance of her special day.

St. Thérèse of Lisieux said shortly before her death, "I will spend my heaven doing good on earth. I will let fall a shower of roses." I never would have thought I would actually receive such a sign.

Yet one day I was in church with my fiancée at the time, now my wife, Dorothy. We were standing in Mass in St. Thomas, and a rose petal came floating down to us. We saw it coming from five or six yards away, gently floating our way. It didn't come straight down from above, but traveled at a diagonal from in front of us until it reached us. I caught it without having to move. Incredible! Where did that come from?

Well, it turned out that Dorothy had been praying a novena to St. Thérèse of Lisieux. When I think of it now, I can hardly believe it happened; yet as it is happening you can do nothing other than accept it. It really is very humbling.

We still have the rose petal framed in our house with a picture of St. Thérèse and other meaningful pictures and icons. It's good to have a meaningful space like that where you can go for prayer. Here is the prayer Dorothy was praying. You may want to give it a try, or find a novena devoted to your own favorite saint.

O Little Thérèse of the Child Jesus, please pick for me a rose from the heavenly gardens and send it to me as a message of love. O Little Flower of Jesus, ask God today to grant the favour I now place with confidence in your hands... (mention specific request). St. Thérèse, help me to always believe as you did, in God's great love for me, so that I might imitate your 'Little Way' each day. Amen

"If a man could pass through Paradise in a dream,
and have a flower presented to him as a pledge
that his soul had really been there,
and if he found
that flower in his hand when he awoke –
Ay! And what then?
–Samuel Taylor Coleridge

Notes:

Day Thirteen

Guided Imagery Meditation

When St. Joan of Arc was going to be burned at the stake for being a witch, they gave her a chance to recant. If she would just admit that the voices she heard were her imagination, they would set her free. She said, "Yes, it was my imagination"... she then added, "But God speaks to me through my imagination!"

God speaks to us in a variety of ways, and our imagination is one of them. Guided imagery meditation is the practice of letting your imagination be directed to lead to some kind of experience of God. Sometimes this is led by a person. You can also buy a CD that will lead the meditation. For today, you can have someone read to you, or perhaps record the meditation so you can listen with your eyes closed. The other option is to simply read a little and then close your eyes to imagine the scene. Then read a little more and imagine again.

In this meditation you will meet Jesus.

As you begin, sit straight in your chair. Your spine should be straight from your tail bone to the top of your head. It is especially important to keep your head straight, not letting your chin drop, which can limit your breathting.

Become aware of each part of your body one by one and consciously let each part of your body relax.

Become aware of your breathing. Take a few deep breathes and relax.

Imagine yourself walking along a beach. You feel the sand in your toes... the gentle breeze in your hair...

As you walk along you see someone up ahead sitting on a log by a small fire...

He calls you over, so you approach the man...

When you get there you realize that it is Jesus... How does he look to you?

He has been expecting you... He welcomes you warmly and gestures for you to be seated...

He asks you about how things are going... and you tell him about your life at this time...

You sense that he knows all about you and what has been going on in your life...

You share with him things you haven't been able to tell anyone...

Jesus then invites you to ask him a question. If you could ask Jesus one question, what would it be? Think before you ask it. Word it with care. When you are ready, ask Jesus the question...

How does Jesus respond?

You sit with Jesus for some time and watch the sun set...

After a while you realize that it is time to leave. He embraces you. You sense his deep abiding love for you. He blesses you and sends you on your way...

... Open your eyes.

Did this way of prayer work for you? Some people will find they have a natural gift for this type of prayer. I led a group in this meditation recently, and one girl went home and did more on her own. She had other questions she wanted to ask Jesus and came back the next day sharing the experience. If you have this gift, it can be a great way to pray.

I have done this exercise many times with groups, and it can lead to good sharing if people are willing to share the question they asked. Many times the question of suffering arises. This is an important question because many lose faith because they cannot believe in a God who allows suffering. Allow me to share a few thoughts on the topic.

Recently a grade eleven student shared with me that she had been going through a rough time, but felt that she was coming through it. This is not so unusual, but what she said next really amazed me. She said that she was even able to look back and be thankful for having gone through this difficult time. That is incredible wisdom!

The great Lebanese American poet and theologian Kahlil Gibran expressed it this way: "I have learned silence from the talkative, toleration from the intolerant, and kindness from the unkind; yet strange, I am ungrateful to those teachers." Saint Paul wrote in Romans: "*We rejoice in our sufferings, because we know that suffering produces perseverance, perseverance, character, and character, hope*" (Rom. 5:3). Suffering makes some bitter, and it makes some better.

Toward the end of the book of Job, which deals with the mystery of suffering, Job concludes that in the end understanding of why there is suffering is beyond him: "*I have been holding forth on matters I cannot understand, on marvels beyond me and my knowledge.*" (42:3b) In the end, he cannot understand, yet he can find consolation in personally and experientially knowing God: "*I knew you then only by hearsay; but now, having seen you with my own eyes, I retract all I have said, and in dust and ashes I repent.*" (42:5-6)

The experience of God assures us that God is good and we have tremendous hope in this. Why there is suffering remains a mystery. Our knowledge and understanding is limited, and we would do well to humbly accept our limitations.

Jesus' teachings are best summed up in the Beatitudes which can be found in Matthew 5. The first beatitude calls us to be poor in spirit, which is to recognize our great need for God. It is to be humble. There is so much we cannot know. To be poor in spirit does not mean to not have much spirit. We should be full of enthusiasm! It means that we know we are weak sinners who have a great need for mercy. Religion can actually be dangerous if it leads us to be self-righteous rather than humble. That is not authentic spirituality. The first beatitude also has to do with not being overly attached to things, or to our own opinions. One sign of an authentic spirituality is a willingness to live simply and to work for a more just world.

For a Christian, the moral code is summed up in these eight beatitudes. My dictionary defines Beatitude as "supreme blessedness or happiness." It is ironic that Jesus' says that the most blessed or extremely happy are the poor, those who mourn, and those who are persecuted. How can this be? In some mysterious way, it is often in the midst of real life struggles, rather than avoiding them, that we find real deep meaning and real joy. We often find God and our real friends at those times. This cannot be explained, but only experienced. The best way to describe the beatitudes is to look at the life of a saint. In Appendix

III I demonstrate the meaning of each beatitude by looking at the life of St. Marguerite d'Youville.

We believe as Christians that Jesus' suffering showed God's perfect love. He gave his life to save us, and revealed to us a God who is perfect love. In some mysterious way our sufferings, when united to his in love, can be redemptive as well. To redeem suffering is to give it some kind of value or purpose. Richard Rohr says that if we don't learn to transform our pain, we will transmit our pain. When I am going through a hard time, nothing helps more than carrying a small crucifix in my pocket so I can hold it in my hand at any time. I am reminded that he is with me; I know goodness always wins in the end, even if not in this life. I know that somehow my suffering united to his has meaning. If you know someone going through a hard time, it can be a great help to give the person a small crucifix to hold.

Notes:

Day Fourteen

Ignatian Prayer with Scripture

This is another form of prayer that uses the imagination. It is a way of praying with scripture called Ignatian contemplation. It is named after St. Ignatius Loyola, the sixteenth century Spanish mystic who was a great teacher of spiritual practices.

Select a scripture passage to be the basis of your prayer – maybe a passage that means a lot to you, maybe the Gospel reading for the upcoming Sunday. Take a few minutes to relax and become aware of the presence of God. Then read the scripture passage you have selected. Read the passage a second time, and pick a character in the story that you identify with. Using your imagination, visualize the scene of the biblical text *with yourself in the scene.*

For example, it may be the story of Jesus healing the blind man from the Gospel of Luke. Can you imagine how exciting it would be to be that man, to have Jesus touch and heal you, to see for the first time? This prayer relies on the use of a vivid imagination, and some people find their gift of imagination makes this an excellent practice for them. The only real rule is not to worry and to let the Lord show himself to you.

St. Thérèse loved using the Gospels in prayer: "Above all, it is the gospels that occupy my mind when I'm at prayer; my soul has so many needs, and yet this is the one thing needful. I'm always finding fresh lights there; hidden meanings which had meant nothing to me hitherto." [19]

You may choose your own Gospel passage to pray with, or use the following, from Matthew 8:1-3.

"After he had come down from the mountain large crowds followed him. A leper now came up and bowed low in front of him. 'Sir,' he said, 'if you want to, you can cure me.' Jesus stretched our his hand, touched him and said, 'Of course I want to! Be cured.' And his leprosy was cured at once."

Here are two other readings you may want to spend time with: Luke 18:35-43; Luke 19:1-10

Notes:

_____

_____

_____

_____

_____

_____

_____

_____

_____

_____

19   Lisieux, *Autobiography*,   218.

Day Fifteen

Lectio Divina

There is an ancient method for praying with scripture called *Lectio Divina*, or divine reading. The roots of scriptural reflection and interpretation go back to Origen in the third century, after whom St. Ambrose taught them to St. Augustine. It was later taught to monks by the founder of Western monasticism, St. Benedict.

You begin by deciding on the scripture passage you will pray with, and then there are four simple steps:

1. Read the passage very slowly and reflectively, pausing wherever a verse strikes you.
2. Read it again and think about what you are reading, reflecting on how it applies to your life.
3. Read it a third time and respond in prayer as you are led by the Spirit.
4. Read it a fourth time simply listening for God's voice deep in your heart. Rest in peaceful silence. You have moved to contemplation, simply being with God.

This method of prayer has been summed up nicely by a Southern Baptist minister who said, "I reads myself full; I thinks myself clear; I prays myself hot; I lets myself cool."

How can you decide which scripture verses to use? The Church sets out readings for each day.   I like to follow these readings, which also follow the liturgical seasons. If you follow these, you will be "on the same page" as a billion other people around the world. I have a small booklet that is mailed to my house each month that has the daily readings. (You can order this at 1-800-387-7164, www.novalis.ca) You can also find the readings on line. (www.catholic.org)

Isaiah 43:1-5 is a beautiful reading you may want to try for today. Hear your loving creator say to you personally:

"But now, thus says Yahweh, who created you, who formed you. Do not be afraid, for I have redeemed you. I have called you by your name, you are mine. Should you pass through the sea, I will be with you; should you walk through fire, you will not be scorched and the fires will not burn you. For I am Yahweh, your God, the Holy One of Israel, your savior… You are precious in my eyes, because you are honored and I love you… Do not be afraid, for I am with you."

Notes:

_____

_____

_____

_____

_____

_____

_____

Day Sixteen

More Lectio Divina

Here is another well-known approach to Lectio Divina. This one has five steps. The first three steps are very helpful for preparing the mind and heart to receive the word in a prayerful way.[20]

Step one - Presence of God: I remind myself that, as I sit here now, God is gazing on me with love and holding me in being. I pause for a moment and think of this.

Step two - Freedom: If God were trying to tell me something, would I know? If God were reassuring me or challenging me, would I notice? I ask for the grace to be free of my own preoccupations and be open to what God may be saying to me.

Step three - Consciousness: How am I really feeling? Knowing that God loves me unconditionally, I can afford to be honest about how I am. I share my feelings openly with the Lord.

---

20 www.sacredspace.ie

Step four - The Word: I take my time to read the Word of God, slowly a few times, allowing myself to dwell on anything that strikes me.

'What man among you with a hundred sheep, losing one, would not leave the ninety-nine in the wilderness and go after the missing one till he found it? And when he found it, would he not joyfully take it on his shoulders and then when he got home, call together his friends and neighbours? 'Rejoice with me,' he would say, 'I have found my sheep that was lost.' In the same way, I tell you, there will be more rejoicing in heaven over one repentant sinner than over ninety-nine virtuous men who have no need of repentance." (Luke 15:4-7)

Step five: Conversation: What is stirring in me as I pray? Am I consoled, troubled? I imagine Jesus at my side and share my feelings with him.

You can also be guided through this process while sitting at your computer at www.sacredspace.ie, a website run by the Jesuits of Ireland.

Notes:

_____

_____

_____

_____

_____

_____

_____

_____

_____

Day Seventeen

The Way of the Cross

In most Catholic churches there are statues and paintings to bring the saints to our consciousness. Besides these, almost every Catholic Church has the Stations of the Cross. These are usually around the walls of the church and show Jesus at various stages as he is carrying the cross and being crucified. We use these to help us meditate on Jesus' self-giving love and sacrificial death.

When we pray with the Stations of the Cross, we stop at each station to contemplate Jesus in his suffering. This is a powerful reminder that Jesus suffered and died for our sins, and also a great consolation to us as we go through our own struggles in life. You may also pray for people you know who are suffering. The usual response at each station is "We adore you O Christ and we bless you – for by your holy cross you have redeemed the world" and then pray the Lord's Prayer, Hail Mary and Glory Be. You may prefer to use prayer booklets that have scripture verses, prayers, and meditations to read as you walk around the Stations of the Cross.

The first station is usually Jesus being condemned by Pontius Pilate and the last one is Jesus being buried in the tomb. There is also a revised stations of the cross that was published by the Vatican's Sacred Congregation for Divine Worship. These Stations of the Cross are as follows:

1. The Last Supper (Luke 22:15-20)
2. In the garden of Gethsemane (Matt. 26:36-38)
3. Before the Sanhedrin (Mark 14:53-55)
4. Before Pontius Pilate (John 18:28-30)
5. The whipping and crowning with thorns (John 19:1-3)
6. The carrying of the cross (John 19:16-17)
7. Simon of Cyrene (Mark 15:21)
8. The Women of Jerusalem (Luke 23:27-31)
9. The stripping and crucifixion (Matt. 27:33-35)
10. The second thief (Luke 23:39-43)
11. Mary and John (John 19:25-27)
12. Death on the cross (John 19:33-34)
13. The new sepulcher (Matt. 27:57-60)
14. The resurrection (Luke 24:1-3)

You may want to go to a Church to pray with the Stations of the Cross. I know of two retreat centers that have the Stations outdoors, which really adds to the experience. If you can't get to a place with physical Stations of the Cross, simply open your Bible and reflect and pray on some or all of the scripture verses.

Notes:

Day Eighteen

Nature

"The best remedy for those who are afraid, lonely or unhappy is to go outside, somewhere where they can be quiet, alone with the heavens, nature and God. Because only then does one feel that all is as it should be and that God wishes to see people happy, amidst the simple beauty of nature." - Anne Frank

Going for a walk in nature can be an excellent way to pray. The following is an excerpt from my mother's writings. It tells of an encounter that took place while preoccupied with an operation she had to have. She had to have a tumor removed and was told by the doctor that she most likely had cancer. She was visiting my sister on the beautiful west coast of Newfoundland. This was her experience:

One day I set out for a walk along the road in the direction of Shallow Bay. It was a beautiful sunny day with just enough wind to ripple the ocean along the coast. Having walked for close on an hour, I sat beneath a tree to rest and breathe the fresh country air. I was totally relaxed, focusing on my breathing, almost at the point of falling asleep. A gust of wind aroused me; I stood and leaned against the tree, then turned and circled its trunk with my arms ... And then I felt like I was becoming a part of that tree, reaching up to the sky, connecting with everybody and everything in the universe. Again, the wind played her role; this time a gentle breeze kissed my face and stirred a feeling within my whole being, and I knew at that moment, clearly and forcefully, that I must not give up, I must not give in to my illness; instead, I needed to muster up courage to face reality and not to deny suffering but to work through it. Then hope will arise. Perhaps this is what some refer to as wordless communication with God. Whatever, I know for sure that it was a life-giving moment for me.

My thoughts drifted to another time of suffering in my life and of my struggle then to get on with living. I remembered the scripture verse from my daughter Janet's funeral Mass that gave me hope and strength to bear such pain – 'With God all things are possible.' I knew in my heart at that moment, standing there in Shallow Bay, my arms reaching toward the sky, that all will be well regardless of what happens. I believed that without pain there can be no joy; both are what makes us know we are alive. A feeling of peace enveloped me and lingered with me as I leisurely walked back to the house. Reflecting on that experience helped me through the next few weeks to see each day as a gift, to live the present joyfully, and to be less anxious about the outcome of my scheduled surgery.

The peace my mother found in nature reminds me of the words of the fourteenth century English mystic, Julian of Norwich: "And all shall be well, and all manner of thing shall be well." With people of faith, there is a sense that the universe is unfolding as it should. Today there is a new theology evolving with our recent knowledge about this unfolding universe.

Today we are aware of about 140 billion galaxies! (Our sun is one of hundreds of millions in our galaxy of the Milky Way.) These galaxies are all moving away from one another in all directions at an ever increasing speed. Scientists have been able to measure backward from today to the time when it all began about fourteen billion years ago. Writers such as Teilhard de Chardin, Thomas Berry, Sr. Mirium MacGillis, Brian Swimme, and Diramuid O'Murchu use the new scientific knowledge to give us a new cosmology, a new creation story. I recently read *Journey of the Universe* by Brian Swimme and Mary Evelyn Tucker, which tells the story of the universe since it began 13.7 billion years ago. By the time I was finished, I had developed an incredible awareness that I am made of the very same material as each and every blade of grass. There is an amazing sense of unity that comes from knowing this story.

Here the story of the cosmos is summarized very nicely by Carmel Higgins, author of *Local Sparks, Cosmic Fire*:

In a nutshell the new story, being told today by mystics, poets, scientists, and theologians alike, goes something like this:

Fourteen billion years ago, from a source of energy the size of a pin-prick, the Universe burst forth from the heart of ultimate Mystery. From the ensuing fireball it began to diversify and to expand in all directions - spewing out frolicking particles, dancing atoms, spiraling galaxies, exploding stars, and whirling planets. On our privileged planet, after molten rock and seething vapors cooled, after rains fell and oceans formed, live cells appeared in the sea and life began. On land, grass, trees, and flowers appeared, followed by reptiles, birds, insects, mammals, and finally... us.

But that's not the end of the story. In the human species, reflective consciousness, freedom, and creativity emerged and the story continued to unfold: Sparked by the same creative energy that gave birth to the Universe, humans invented language, made tools, and discovered fire. They created villages, communities, and great civilizations. They created rituals to celebrate life and death.

They wrote sacred books. They discovered healing medicine, atoms, DNA, quantum theory, and went to the moon and back. Humans are innately spirited and creative, and continue to unfold the story to this day."[21]

You can see more on this amazing story at www.journeyoftheuniverse.org. It can be very humbling to think of the size of the universe. Nature has a lot to teach us. St. Seraphim of Sarov (b. 1759) wrote the following on how nature can teach us to pray. This may inspire your prayer today. You may also want to make time to get out and experience nature if you can.

When you pray, be like the mountain
    In stillness, in silence,
    Thoughts rooted in eternity.
    Do nothing; just sit, just be,
And you will harvest the fruit of your prayer

When you pray, be like the flower
    Reaching up to the sun,
    Straight stemmed like a column.
    Be open, ready to accept all things without fear
And you will not lack light on your way

When you pray, be like the ocean,
    With stillness in its depths,
    The waves ebbing and flowing
    Have calm in your heart,
And evil thoughts will flee of their own accord

When you pray, remember the breath
    That made us people, living beings;
    From God it comes, to God it returns.
    Blend the Word and prayer with the flow of life
And nothing will come between you and the Giver of Life

---

21 Carmel Higgins, *Cosmic Fire/Local Sparks: My Journey into the Universe Story*. ISBN 0-9734164 Contact Higgins@nb.sympatico.ca

When you pray, be like the bird,
      Endlessly singing before the Creator,
      Its song rising like incense.
Pray like the turtle dove
    And you will never lose heart.

Notes:

Day Nineteen

The Liturgy of the Hours

The Liturgy of the Hours, also known as the Divine Office, is a very easy and relaxing way to pray. The Liturgy of the Hours takes about ten to fifteen minutes as we pray the psalms in the morning, evening and night. Priests, nuns and brothers are required to pray the Liturgy of the Hours, but lay people are encouraged to as well. Catholic religious in every time zone around the world pray the Divine Office many times a day, so somewhere in the world the Church is *always* offering up this prayer. As a body we fulfill the command to *"pray at all times"* (Thes. 5:17).

The Divine Office is mostly made up of the psalms. Morning and evening prayer includes three psalms and night prayer includes one. Why so much emphasis on the psalms? The psalms are a collection of prayers, and Jesus prayed the psalms. We see in the Gospel of Mark after the Last Supper, it says, *"After psalms had been sung they left for the Mount of Olives"* (Mark 14:26). According to the Gospels, even Jesus's last words on the cross were a prayer taken from the psalms: *"My God, my God, why have you deserted me?"* (Ps 22:1, Mark 15:34) and *"Father, into your hands I commit my spirit"* (Ps 31:5, Luke 23:46). If we live praying the psalms, they become a part of us and we may even have the good fortune to, like Christ, die praying them. St. Paul calls on his readers to *"Sing the words and tunes of the psalms and hymns when you are together, and go on singing and chanting to the Lord in your hearts."* (Eph 5:19)

St. Thérèse of Lisieux enjoyed praying the Divine Office and wrote that she found no consolation in any other prayer books: "I recite the Divine Office with a great sense of unworthiness, but apart from that I can't face the strain of hunting about in books for these splendid prayers – it makes my head spin." [22]

You can buy a prayer book that gives psalms and scripture readings for morning, evening and night prayer from any Catholic book store. It is an excellent investment. If you prefer, there's an app for that.

You will find that the Divine Office incorporates many of the elements of prayer discussed earlier: vocal prayer, the Glory Be after psalms, praying with scripture, the Lord's Prayer, and petitions. Evening prayer includes the Magnificat, and night prayer contains an awareness examen.

I have chosen a collection of prayers from the Divine Office so you can try it for today's prayer. This can be used as morning prayer or evening prayer. Appendix one contains a night prayer for each day of the week, which you may want to use as part of your daily prayer routine in the future. To pray the Divine Office, you simply read through in a prayerful and reflective way. Give it a try.

Take your time and enjoy the Divine Office. It can be very relaxing. It is traditional to begin with the words, "God, come to my assistance – Lord, make haste to help me." This is known as the invitatory. We begin by asking God to help us pray. It is very liberating to let go and let God guide this time of prayer.

Invitatory:

God, come to my assistance.
Lord, make haste to help me.
Glory to the Father, and to the Son, and to the Holy Spirit,
As it was in the beginning, is now, and will be forever. Amen.

Antiphon: I look to you, O God, to be my strength this day.

---

22 Lisieux, *Autobiography,* 289.

Psalm 63:2-9
A soul thirsting for God

Whoever has left the darkness of sin, yearns for God.

O God, you are my God, for you I long;
For you my soul is thirsting.
My body pines for you
Like a dry, weary land without water.
So I gaze on you in the sanctuary
To see your strength and your glory.

For your love is better than life,
My lips will speak your praise.
So I will bless you all my life,
In your name I will lift up my hands.
My soul shall be filled as with a banquet,
My mouth shall praise you with joy.

On my bed I remember you.
On you I muse through the night
For you have been my help;
In the shadow of your wings I rejoice.
My soul clings to you;
Your right hand holds me fast.

Glory to the Father, and to the Son, and to the Holy Spirit,
As it was in the beginning, is now, and will be forever. Amen.

Antiphon: I look to you, O God, to be my strength this day.

Reading   Colossians 3:15-17

May the peace of Christ reign in your hearts, because it is for this that you were called together as parts of one body. Always be thankful. Let the message of Christ, in all its richness, find a home with you. Teach each other, and advise each other, in all wisdom. With gratitude in your hearts sing psalms and hymns and inspired songs to God; and never say or do anything except in the name of the Lord Jesus, giving thanks to God the Father through him.

Responsory

I shall know the fullness of joy when I see your face, O Lord.
Fulfillment and endless peace in our presence – when I see your face O Lord.
Glory to the Father, and to the Son, and to the Holy Spirit.
I shall know the fullness of joy when I see your face, O Lord.

If praying in the morning, pray the following Canticle of Zachariah. If praying in the evening, pray the Magnificat from day eight.

Blessed be the Lord, the God of Israel;
He has come to his people and set them free.
He has raised up for us a mighty savior,
Born of the house of his servant David.
Through his holy prophets he promised of old
That he would save us from our enemies,
From the hands of all who hate us.
He promised to show mercy to our fathers
And to remember his holy covenant.
This was the oath he swore to our father Abraham:
To set us free from the hands of our enemies,
Free to worship him without fear,
Holy and righteous in his sight all the days of our life.
You, my child, shall be called the prophet of the Most High;
For you will go before the Lord to prepare his way,
To give his people knowledge of salvation
by the forgiveness of their sins.
In the tender compassion of our God
 the dawn from an high shall break upon us,
To shine on those who dwell in darkness and the shadow of death,
And to guide our feet into the way of peace.

Glory to the Father, and to the Son, and to the Holy Spirit,
As it was in the beginning, is now, and will be forever. Amen.

Petitions

Christ came and gave himself up to purify his people, to make of them an acceptable offering, a band of disciples to continue his good work. With fervent devotion let us call upon him: *Lord, have mercy*

For your holy Church – that all her children may be born again into a new life: *Lord, have mercy*

For the poor, for prisoners and for refugees – may they find you, the incarnate Son of God, in our love: *Lord, have mercy*

That our joy may be full – and that we may marvel at the Father's gift, which he has given us in you: *Lord, have mercy*

That your servants who have died with the knowledge of your birth may see your face – and that night may fall upon them no more: *Lord, have mercy*

Our Father...

Prayer

Lord Jesus Christ,
You have given your followers
An example of gentleness and humility,
A task that is easy, a burden that is light.
Help us to follow your example of gentleness and humility
And keep us in your peace.
Amen.

Conclusion

May the Lord bless us, protect us from all evil and bring us to everlasting life. Amen[23]

23 Excerpts from the English translation of *The Liturgy of the Hours* ©1974, International Commission on English in the Liturgy Corporation. All rights reserved. The English translation of the *Gloria Patri*, *Benedictus*, and *Magnificat* by the International Consultation on English Texts.

Notes:

_____

_____

_____

_____

_____

_____

_____

_____

Day Twenty

Centering Prayer

"I am the vine, you are the branches. Whoever remains in me, with me in him, bears fruit in plenty; for cut off from me you can do nothing" (John 15:5).

Centering prayer is a simple resting in God's presence. This is pure contemplation, being with God. It is both extremely simple and extremely rewarding. It's all about being attentive to the presence of God.

To begin centering prayer, simply sit still with an upright posture. You sit in a chair so your two feet are on the floor and place your hands on your lap. Take a minute to relax and quiet yourself down. Take a few deep breathes. Choose a prayer word: peace, love, God, whatever it might be. Then, repeat the word over and over in a relaxed way, perhaps in conjunction with your breathing. This is called a mantra and is a soothing way to become centered and grounded in God. As the psalmist says, *"Be still, and know that I am God"* (Ps. 46:10). Spiritual writers[24] suggest we do this for twenty minutes in the morning and again in the afternoon. You may want to begin with five minutes if this is your first time.

St. Franics used to pray "my God and my all" all through the night. To get a sense of this I like to think of the universe story, which began 13.7 billion years ago. I think of God who existed even before that! I am reminded that God is infinitely bigger than anything I can conceive of or worry about, and yet intimately involved in the tiniest detail of my life. My God and my all.

Some like to focus on their breathing as they do this prayer. Another good thought that dissolves our egos is that God is like the air that is all around us and this is the same air we breathe within us. God surrounds us and is within us. My God and my all.

Another variation is the Jesus prayer, which dates back to the fifth century: "Lord Jesus Christ, Son of God, have mercy on me, a sinner." You say this prayer repeatedly in rhythm with your breathing. If this all sounds too easy, don't worry. The essence of centering prayer is its simplicity.

John Main (1926-1982) was a Benedictine priest who taught this way of prayer, using the word maranatha as the mantra. It is the last word in the Bible and it means, Come, Lord Jesus. Here is a paragraph from his book, *Moment of Christ*:

"The essence is simply learning to say that word, to recite it, to sound it, from the beginning to the end. It is utterly simple — say it like this: 'Ma-ra-na-tha'. Four equally stressed syllables. Most people say the word in conjunction with their breathing, but that isn't the essence. The essence requires that you say it right throughout your prayer time. The speed should be something that is fairly slow, fairly rhythmical — 'Ma-ra-na-tha'. You have a word, and you say your word, and you remain still."[25]

In this prayer the Spirit is praying in us: *"For when we cannot choose words in order to pray properly, the Spirit himself expresses our plea in a way that could never be put into words"* (Rom. 8:26). You may just want to focus on your breathing, with your breathing being a sign of the Holy Spirit within you.

The intent of this prayer the very same intent that I said of the Lord's prayer on day one, when I said that "praying this prayer is to choose to consent to God's reign in your heart." You might even choose as your mantra "Your kingdom

---

24 Basil Pennington and Thomas Keating have written many books and articles on this form of prayer.

25 John Main, OSB, *Moment of Christ, The Path of Meditation*, (London: Darton, Longman & Todd Ltd., 1984) 1.

come" or "Your will be done." The first letter of John says that *God is love* and to pray for God's reign is to pray for the reign of love in your heart. You may choose the word love as your mantra. The idea of spending twenty minutes is that it takes time for God's spirit of love to really take root in our hearts. We pray that we may *"know the love of Christ which is beyond all knowledge"* and that our lives will be *"rooted in love and built on love."* (Eph. 3:17-19)

It really is an extremely simple form of prayer. Go ahead, give it a try. You can try it for as long as you choose. It is a good idea to decide how many minutes you would like to do it for and then do what you have committed to. Don't worry if you find your mind wandering; it's quite natural. Each time you notice your mind wandering, simply return to your prayer word. Each time you do you are saying that God is bigger and more powerful than whatever it is you were thinking about. Think about God fourteen billion years ago and everything gets put in perspective!

I find that when I am faithful to this prayer twice a day I tend to notice a lot more "coincidences" in my life.

Notes:

Day Twenty-one

Journaling

You may have been journaling throughout this book as you evaluated your experience of each form of prayer. Journaling can be a great way to clarify our thoughts, and can be considered a form of prayer. It can be used in conjunction with other forms of prayer, such as the examen awareness or praying with scripture. Another good time to write is when you feel there is a lot on your mind and you need to figure things out or make an important decision. If you have an important decision to make, prayer is crucial. As part of the process it may help to make a chart in which you list the reasons for and against a few different choices.[26]

Go to university after high school		Join the Navy for a year before university	
pros	cons	pros	cons

---

26 For more on this topic, see *Decision Making* by John Veltri, www.jesuits.ca/orientations

This is all part of figuring out or discerning God's will for us. It is a way of working at the line from the Lord's Prayer, "Thy will be done." At a convention in Phoenix in 2009 Pope Benedict XVI sent the following message to those gathered: "Young people, if they know how to pray, can be trusted to know what to do with God's call." This book teaches how to pray so that you can hear God's call. *Appendix II* contains an excellent article that goes into more depth about how to discern a major calling in life, such as the choice between marriage, single life, priesthood or religious life.

But right now you are invited to make a more immediate choice about how you might continue to practice prayer in your life. Assuming you believe it would be a good idea to pray, next you have to decide which of the ways of prayer you will practice. Since this is the last of the twenty-one days, right now would be a good time to write about which forms of prayer you think are best for you.

Reflect on your experience of prayer on each of the twenty-one days. Review any journaling you did at the end of each chapter. Are there any types of prayer that really worked well for you? Were there any significant insights?

Now it is time to make some choices. What do you think should be your habit of prayer? What type of prayer will you commit to, when, and where? Make it our own. Which forms of prayer are you drawn to? Perhaps you will begin your day with one of the types of Lectio Divina and end each day with an awareness examen. Perhaps you will decide to pray the Divine Office from the Appendix every night before bed. Perhaps you feel called to try centering prayer in the morning and evening.

It may help to go on a retreat to really develop a rule of life and to seek out a spiritual director who can give you some guidance. You may want to ask your parish priest. If you don't know someone you can ask, you may want to try www.sdiworld.org. Spiritual Directors International is an amazing site that helps you connect with qualified spiritual directors.

It is important to determine a place where you will pray and to decide on a time of day when you will do it. For today's prayer, take some time to pray for guidance and to think. Then write down *where, when, and how* you plan to pray.

Notes:

_____

_____

_____

_____

_____

_____

_____

_____

_____

_____

Conclusion

A disciple asked his teacher of prayer:
"Is there anything I can do to make myself more enlightened?"
"As little as you can do to make the sun rise in the morning."
"Then of what use are the spiritual exercises you teach?"
"To make sure you are not asleep when the sun begins to rise."

The experience of God's Spirit of life and love is a gift always available to us. Gerald May wrote the following about our role in receiving this gift: "When it presents itself to us our primary role is to be wakeful and willing, not necessarily to create the opportunity, but to be open to respond to it when it is given. My sense is that such opportunities occur very frequently, perhaps many times each day. We miss most of them because we are so noisy in our minds or so attached in our hearts – and so self-important in our egos – that we are dulled and blinded. It is one role of spiritual practice, of prayer and meditation, fasting and service, to wake up to more of these graced moments and to be more flexibly responsive to them when they occur." [27]

---

27 Gerald G. May, M.D., *Will and Spirit,* (San Francisco, Harper, 1982), 308.

Spontaneous prayer is great, but a plan for a prayer life is important as well. It's like friendship – chance encounters happen, but if you want to sustain a friendship you make it a priority and make plans to get together.

People have to decide for themselves what practices would best help their spiritual life. The main idea here is that a spiritual life requires some discipline to develop a habit of daily prayer. It has been said that discipline is the ability to do what ought to be done, when it ought to be done, whether you feel like it or not.

The word *disciple* has discipline as its root. Ronald Rolheiser wrote an amazing book called *The Shattered Lantern – Rediscovering a Felt Presence of God.* It states quite frankly that "We live in an age of unbelief."[28] The book discusses reasons for this loss of faith and suggests ways to recover "the ancient instinct for astonishment." In summarizing his thoughts on the last page of the book he says, "Blessed are those whose discipleship includes the discipline of regular prayer; they shall know that it is in God that they live and move and have their being."[29] This book is an attempt to take this suggestion to the next step – to discuss how it is we can practice this advice that so many of the saints have given.

I remember an economics high school teacher who had done very well for himself financially. It was said of him that "there was a teacher who lived what he taught." This teacher told me that he paid attention to the stock market and worked at it about forty-five minutes a day. Good for him. I hope he does well with the money. But I wish we saw the pursuit of God as at least as important, and had the discipline to give it as much time and effort.

Or think about how much time we are willing to work on our physical fitness or education. Why is it that we don't give as much effort to developing our spiritual lives? I really believe it is because of a lack of faith. Why pray if we do not have faith? On the other hand, how can we have faith, a relationship with God, if we do *not* pray? There comes a point when we have to make a choice. If you have faith even the size of a mustard seed, that is enough to get you started. If you want to grow in the spiritual life, there comes a point when you have to make the leap of faith – to start praying.

I once asked a group of students whether or not they believed in God. As usual, almost all said they did. Then I asked *why* they believed in God. The answers varied: "We had to come from somewhere." "Because I was brought up this way." Then one girl said, "Because God answers my prayers." I immediately

---

28 Ronald Rolheiser, *The Shattered Lantern*, (New York, The Crossroad Publishing Company, 2001), 17.
29 Ibid, 204.

said to myself, "That is an answer I would want my own children and my students to be able to say." That answer suggests that there has been some kind of *experience*. There is something going on between you and God; there is a relationship, what we would call a spiritual life.

I believe that there is a great need for private prayer if we are to grow to know God. Yet it is necessary to have the support of a community as well. The sixteenth century Spanish mystic St. John of the Cross said that "The virtuous soul that is alone and without a master is like a lone burning coal. It will grow colder rather than hotter." It is a good practice to have a spiritual director, a person you can speak to about your prayer and faith life. The sacrament of reconciliation is an excellent practice as well. Enjoying the Sabbath as a day of rest and going to Mass to hear the Word of God is very helpful as well. My pastor growing up changed my life because he gave of his very self as he preached from experience and from a heart steeped in deep reflection and prayer.

The sacrament of the Eucharist is absolutely essential for a Catholic. Right after receiving Eucharist is when I feel closest to God. When I go to pray after receiving Eucharist, I tend to lose myself in prayer. The words come to mind, "*I live not with my own life but with the life of Christ who lives in me.*" (Gal. 2:20)

Henry Nouwen says that we usually set out to do things; then, when we can't get it all done alone, we look for help from others; when that doesn't work, we cry out to God for help. We need to turn that around: Start with solitude and prayer, out of which we have the depth to be able to develop true intimacy and community, and then we can go forward together in community and do our work in the world. And God knows there's lots to be done to make this a more just, loving, and peaceful world!

When I was in my twenties, I had the privilege to work in the developing island nation of Dominica for four years. It is a beautiful country about fifteen miles wide by thirty miles long and has a population of about 85,000. I was teaching there with the Irish Christian Brothers.

You never know how much you can miss home until you go away. On one particular night I was feeling a bit down and decided to go for a walk. I remember someone asked me where I was going and my reply was one word: "nowhere."

As I wandered through town, I came across a boy from the school where I taught. He was only in grade three and it was ten o'clock at night! I said, "Where are you going?" and his reply caught me off guard: "Nowhere."

So we went nowhere together for a while. He followed me back to the house where the brothers were praying the Divine Office together. We could see and hear them from the parking lot where we were sitting outside the chapel.

Julian asked me, "Why do you pray?" I said, "Well, because we love God and want to thank him for all his blessings." Then he asked, "Can I have a bread?" I was thinking that this little guy should be getting home, so I said no. Then he said a line I will never forget: "Ah! See how you is! You say you love God – then you no give me a bread!"

Needless to say, I got him some food. After we had a little something to eat, I walked him home and was shocked to see his living conditions. He was staying with his very elderly grandparents, whose bed took up practically the whole shack where they lived.

I am happy to say that with the amazing generosity of a certain lady called Nurse Laurant, Julian's conditions improved quite a bit. I was also able to teach him to read and write. I'm glad I did because I have thoroughly enjoyed getting many letters from him and hearing that he is doing so well now as a successful young man.

He taught me an important lesson: if we say we are people of faith, then it has to show itself in action. There's something seriously wrong in this world where there are so many without basic necessities while others have more than they need. Many just don't seem to care or feel any sense of responsibility for others or for the planet. It's a simple concept, expressed repeatedly in scripture: *"If a person was rich enough in this world's goods saw that one of his brothers was in need but closed his heart to him, how could the love of God be living in him"* (1 Jn. 4:17).[30]

We are all radically related. If you come to recognize God within, you are far more likely to recognize God in others as well, and goodness, kindness and generosity will flow from that realization. G.K. Chesterton said that "Christianity has not been tried and found wanting; it has been found difficult and never tried".

We can't change the world by ourselves, but that doesn't mean we should not do what we can. Working with good organizations trying to bring about real long term change is important as well. My favorite organization is *Development and Peace* because they provide relief in times of disaster and work for long term systemic change as well. (www.devp.org)

And of course this kindness we are called to practice starts right where we are. There are many opportunities for kindness around you right now. There is no need to go overseas. I heard a story at church recently that illustrates the point. A young boy was dying from cancer. An uncle who was a priest would visit him faithfully every day. One day the boy asked his uncle, "What will happen when I

---

30 An outstanding book I recommend on this topic is called *The Life You Can Save; Acting Now to End World Poverty*, by Peter Singer. (New York: Random House, 2009)

die?" The priest said, "You will see God." Then he asked the boy, "Are you afraid to die?" The boy said, "If God is as kind as you, then what do I have to be afraid of?"

That is Christianity in a nutshell. It is good news of an extremely merciful God revealed to us in the life and teachings of Jesus. This God who became flesh by the Holy Spirit continues to become flesh in us who are formed and led by that same Spirit.

I began this book with the statement that you are free. You were invited to make a choice to take some time to pray and learn about various spiritual practices. These practices are important if we are to feed the good wolf, if we are to nurture *love, joy, peace, patience, kindness, goodness, faithfulness, gentleness, and self-control* (Galatians 5:22). To make the choice to nurture these through a serious commitment to prayer would be a rare choice indeed.

In the Gospel of John there is a story of a woman who encounters Jesus. She is overwhelmed by the experience and goes off to tell the whole town about him. They believed in him on the strength of her testimony and so they came and met him for themselves. After their own encounter with him they said to the woman, "*Now we no longer believe because of what you told us; we have heard him ourselves and we know that he really is the savior of the world.*" (John 4:42) It is my hope that the ways of prayer in this book will lead you to your own encounter. What happens from here is between you and God. You are free.

Appendix I – Divine Office Night Prayer

Sunday

Introduction

> God, come to my assistance.
> Lord, make haste to help me.
>
> Glory to the Father, and to the Son, and to the Holy Spirit,
> As it was in the beginning, is now, and will be forever. Amen.

Examination of Conscience:

Pray the prayer of the blind man, "Lord, that I might see."
Then close your eyes. Relax and wait. See what comes to mind from your day.
Pray about what comes to mind – *"Give your cares to God, for God cares for you"* (1
Pet. 5:7). (Or if praying with someone, share your insight/memory and then
begin the rest of night prayer.)

Antiphon: Night holds no terrors for me sleeping under God's wings.

Psalm 91

He who dwells in the shelter of the Most High
And abides in the shade of the Almighty
Says to the Lord: "My refuge,
My stronghold, my God in whom I trust!"

It is he who will free you from the snare
Of the fowler who seeks to destroy you;
He will conceal you with his pinions
And under his wings you will find refuge.

You will not fear the terror of the night
Nor the arrow that flies by day,
Nor the plague that prowls in the darkness
Nor the scourge that lays waste at noon.

A thousand may fall at your side,
Ten thousand fall at your right,
You it will never approach;
His faithfulness is buckler and shield.

Your eyes have only to look
To see how the wicked are repaid,
You who have said: "Lord, my refuge!"
And have made the Most High your dwelling.

Upon you no evil shall fall,
No plague approach where you dwell.
For you has he commanded his angels,
to keep you in all your ways.

They shall bear you upon their hands
Lest you strike your foot against a stone.
On the lion and the viper you will tread
And trample the young lion and the dragon.

Since he clings to me in love, I will free him;
Protect him for he knows my name.
When he calls I shall answer: "I am with you."
I shall save him in distress and give him glory.

With length of life I will content him;
I shall let him see my saving power.

Glory to the Father, and to the Son, and to the Holy Spirit,
As it was in the beginning, is now, and will be forever. Amen.

Psalm prayer: Lord Jesus Christ, when tempted by the devil, you remained loyal to your Father whose angels watched over you at his command. Guard your Church and keep us safe from the plague of sin so that we may remain loyal to the day we enjoy your salvation and your glory.

A reading from the Book of Revelation (22:4-5)
They will look upon his face, and his name will be on their foreheads. Night will be no more, nor will they need light from lamp or sun, for the Lord God shall give them light, and they shall reign forever and ever.

Responsory:

Into your hands, Lord, I commend my spirit.
  - Into your hands, Lord, I commend my spirit.
You have redeemed us, Lord God of truth.
  - I commend my spirit.
Glory to the Father, to the Son, and to the Holy Spirit
  - Into your hands, Lord, I commend my spirit.

Antiphon: Protect us, Lord, as we stay awake; watch over us as we sleep, that awake, we may keep watch with Christ, and asleep, rest in peace.

Lord, now you let your servant go in peace;
Your word has been fulfilled:
My own eyes have seen the salvation
Which you have prepared in the sight of every people:

A light to reveal you to the nations
And the glory of your people Israel. (Luke 2:29-32)

Glory to the Father, and to the Son, and to the Holy Spirit,
As it was in the beginning, is now, and will be forever. Amen.

Protect us, Lord, as we stay awake; watch over us as we sleep, that awake, we may keep watch with Christ, and asleep, rest in peace.

Prayer:

Lord,
We have celebrated today
The mystery of the rising of Christ to new life.
May we now rest in your peace,
Safe from all that could harm us,
And rise again refreshed and joyful,
To praise you throughout another day.
We ask this through Christ our Lord.

Conclusion:

May the all-powerful Lord grant us a restful night and a peaceful death.
- Amen.

Hail Mary

Hail Mary, full of grace,
The Lord is with you!
Blessed are you among women,
And blessed is the fruit of your womb, Jesus.
Holy Mary, Mother of God,
Pray for us sinners,
Now and at the hour of our death.

Monday

Introduction

God, come to my assistance.
Lord, make haste to help me.

Glory to the Father, and to the Son, and to the Holy Spirit,
As it was in the beginning, is now, and will be forever. Amen.

Examination of Conscience:

Pray the prayer of the blind man, "Lord, that I might see."
Then close your eyes. Relax and wait. See what comes to mind from your day.
Pray about what comes to mind. — *"Give your cares to God, for God cares for you"*(1
Pet. 5:7). (Or if praying with someone, share your insight/memory and then
begin the rest of night prayer.)

Antiphon: O Lord, our God, unwearied is your love for us.

Psalm 86

Turn your ear, O Lord, and give answer
For I am poor and needy.
Preserve my life, for I am faithful:
Save the servant who trusts in you.

You are my God; have mercy on me, Lord,
For I cry to you all the day long.
Give joy to your servant, O Lord,
For to you I lift up my soul.

O Lord, you are good and forgiving,
Full of love to all who call.
Give heed, O Lord, to my prayer
And attend to the sound of my voice.

In the day of distress I will call
And surely you will reply.
Among the gods there is none like you, O Lord;
Nor work to compare with yours.

All the nations shall come to adore you
And glorify your name, O Lord:
For you are great and do marvelous deeds,
You who alone are God.

Show me, Lord, your way
So that I may walk in your truth.
Guide my heart to fear your name.

I will praise you, Lord my God, with all my heart
And glorify your name for ever;
For your love to me has been great:
You have saved me from the depths of the grave.

The proud have risen against me;
Ruthless men seek my life:

To you they pay no heed.

But you, God of mercy and compassion,
Slow to anger, O Lord,
Abounding in love and truth,
Turn and take pity on me.
O give your strength to your servant
And save your handmaid's son.
Show me a sign of your favor
That my foes may see to their shame
That you console me and give me your help.

Glory to the Father, and to the Son, and to the Holy Spirit,
As it was in the beginning, is now, and will be forever. Amen.

Psalm prayer: God of mercy and goodness, when Christ called out to you in torment, you heard him and gave him victory over death because of his love for you. We already know the affection you have for us; fill us with a greater love of your name and we will proclaim you more boldly before all and happily lead them to celebrate your glory.

A reading from Paul's first letter to the Thessalonians (5:9-10)

For God did not destine us for wrath, but to gain salvation through our Lord Jesus Christ, who died for us, so that whether we are awake or asleep we may live together with him.

Responsory

Into your hands, Lord, I commend my spirit.
   - Into your hands, Lord, I commend my spirit.
You have redeemed us, Lord God of truth.
   - I commend my spirit.
Glory to the Father, to the Son, and to the Holy Spirit
   - Into your hands, Lord, I commend my spirit.

Antiphon: Protect us, Lord, as we stay awake; watch over us as we sleep, that awake, we may keep watch with Christ, and asleep, rest in peace.

Lord, now you let your servant go in peace;
Your word has been fulfilled:
My own eyes have seen the salvation
Which you have prepared in the sight of every people:
A light to reveal you to the nations
And the glory of your people Israel (Luke 2:29-32).

Glory to the Father, and to the Son, and to the Holy Spirit,
As it was in the beginning, is now, and will be forever. Amen.

Protect us, Lord, as we stay awake; watch over us as we sleep, that awake, we may keep watch with Christ, and asleep, rest in peace.

Prayer:

Lord,
Give our bodies restful sleep
And let the work we have done today
Bear fruit in eternal life.
We ask this through Christ our Lord.

Conclusion:

May the all-powerful Lord grant us a restful night and a peaceful death.
- Amen.

Hail Mary

Hail Mary, full of grace,
The Lord is with you!
Blessed are you among women,
And blessed is the fruit of your womb, Jesus.
Holy Mary, Mother of God,
Pray for us sinners,
Now and at the hour of our death.

Tuesday

Introduction

God, come to my assistance.
Lord, make haste to help me.

Glory to the Father, and to the Son, and to the Holy Spirit,
As it was in the beginning, is now, and will be forever. Amen.

Examination of Conscience:

Pray the prayer of the blind man, "Lord, that I might see."
Then close your eyes. Relax and wait. See what comes to mind from your day.

Pray about what comes to mind. — *"Give your cares to God, for God cares for you"*(1 Pet. 5:7). (Or if praying with someone, share your insight/memory and then begin the rest of night prayer)

Antiphon: Do not hide your face from me; in you I put my trust.

Psalm 143:1-11

Lord, listen to my prayer:
Turn your ear to my appeal.
You are faithful, you are just; give answer.
Do not call your servant to judgment
For no one is just in your sight.

The enemy pursues my soul;
He has crushed my life to the ground;
He has made me dwell in darkness
Like the dead, long forgotten.
Therefore my spirit fails;
My heart is numb within me.

I remember the days that are past:
I ponder all your words.
I muse on what your hand has wrought
And to you I stretch out my hands.
Like a parched land my soul thirsts for you.

Lord, make haste and answer;
For my spirit fails within me.
Do not hide your face
Lest I become like those in the grave.

In the morning let me know your love
For I put my trust in you.
Make me know the way I should walk:
To you I lift up my soul.

Rescue me, Lord, from my enemies;
I have fled to you for refuge.
Teach me to do your will
For you, O Lord, are my God.
Let your good spirit guide me

In ways that are level and smooth.

For your name's sake, Lord, save my life;
In your justice save my soul from distress.

Glory to the Father, and to the Son, and to the Holy Spirit,
As it was in the beginning, is now, and will be forever. Amen.

Psalm prayer: Lord Jesus, early in the morning of your resurrection, you made your love known and brought the first light of dawn to those who dwell in darkness. Your death has opened a path for us. Do not enter into judgment with your servants; let your good Spirit guide us together into the land of justice.

A reading from the first letter of Peter (5:8-9a)
Be sober and vigilant. Your opponent the devil is prowling around like a roaring lion looking for someone to devour. Resist him, steadfast in faith.

Responsory

Into your hands, Lord, I commend my spirit.
   - Into your hands, Lord, I commend my spirit.
You have redeemed us, Lord God of truth.
   - I commend my spirit.
Glory to the Father, to the Son, and to the Holy Spirit
   - Into your hands, Lord, I commend my spirit.

Antiphon: Protect us, Lord, as we stay awake; watch over us as we sleep, that awake, we may keep watch with Christ, and asleep, rest in peace.

Lord, now you let your servant go in peace;
Your word has been fulfilled:
My own eyes have seen the salvation
Which you have prepared in the sight of every people:
A light to reveal you to the nations
And the glory of your people Israel (Luke 2:29-32).

Glory to the Father, and to the Son, and to the Holy Spirit,
As it was in the beginning, is now, and will be forever. Amen.

Protect us, Lord, as we stay awake; watch over us as we sleep, that awake,
we may keep watch with Christ, and asleep, rest in peace.

Prayer:

Lord,
Fill this night with your radiance.
May we sleep in peace and rise with joy
To welcome the light of a new day in your name.
We ask this through Christ our Lord.

Conclusion:

May the all-powerful Lord grant us a restful night and a peaceful death.
- Amen.

Hail Mary

Hail Mary, full of grace,
The Lord is with you!
Blessed are you among women,
And blessed is the fruit of your womb, Jesus.
Holy Mary, Mother of God,
Pray for us sinners,
Now and at the hour of our death.

Wednesday

Introduction

God, come to my assistance.
Lord, make haste to help me.

Glory to the Father, and to the Son, and to the Holy Spirit,
As it was in the beginning, is now, and will be forever. Amen.

Examination of Conscience:

Pray the prayer of the blind man, "Lord, that I might see."
Then close your eyes. Relax and wait. See what comes to mind from your day. Pray about what comes to mind. — *"Give your cares to God, for God cares for you"*(1 Peter 5:7). (Or if praying with someone, share your insight/memory and then begin the rest of night prayer)

Antiphon: Lord God, be my refuge and my strength.

Psalm 31:1-6

Jesus knew this psalm and prayed from it on the cross: *"Father, into your hands I commend my spirit."* (Luke 23:46)

In you, O Lord, I take refuge.
Let me never be put to shame.
In your justice, set me free,
Hear me and speedily rescue me.

Be a rock of refuge for me,
A mighty stronghold to save me,
For you are my rock, my stronghold.
For your name's sake, lead me and guide me.

Release me from the snares they have hidden
For you are my refuge, Lord.
Into your hands I commend my spirit.
It is you who will redeem me, Lord.

Glory to the Father, and to the Son, and to the Holy Spirit,
As it was in the beginning, is now, and will be forever. Amen.

Psalm prayer: Full of trust we run to you, Lord, and put our lives into your hands. You are our strength in times of trouble and our refuge along the way. May you be our joy at the turning points of life and our reward at its end.

A reading from Paul's letter to the Ephesians (4:26-27)

Even if you are angry, you must not sin; never let the sun set on your anger or else you will give the devil a foothold.

Responsory

Into your hands, Lord, I commend my spirit.
>   - Into your hands, Lord, I commend my spirit.

You have redeemed us, Lord God of truth.
>   - I commend my spirit.

Glory to the Father, to the Son, and to the Holy Spirit
>   - Into your hands, Lord, I commend my spirit.

Antiphon: Protect us, Lord, as we stay awake; watch over us as we sleep, that awake, we may keep watch with Christ, and asleep, rest in peace.

Lord, now you let your servant go in peace;
Your word has been fulfilled:
My own eyes have seen the salvation
Which you have prepared in the sight of every people:
A light to reveal you to the nations
And the glory of your people Israel (Luke 2:29-32).

Glory to the Father, and to the Son, and to the Holy Spirit,
As it was in the beginning, is now, and will be forever. Amen.

Protect us, Lord, as we stay awake; watch over us as we sleep, that awake, we may keep watch with Christ, and asleep, rest in peace.

Prayer:

Lord Jesus Christ,
You have given your followers
An example of gentleness and humility,
A task that is easy, a burden that is light.
Accept the prayers and work of this day,
And give us the rest that will strengthen us

To render more faithful service to you
Who live and reign for ever and ever.

Conclusion:

May the all-powerful Lord grant us a restful night and a peaceful death.
- Amen.

Hail Mary

Hail Mary, full of grace,
The Lord is with you!
Blessed are you among women,
And blessed is the fruit of your womb, Jesus.
Holy Mary, Mother of God,
Pray for us sinners,
Now and at the hour of our death.

Thursday

Introduction

God, come to my assistance.
Lord, make haste to help me.

Glory to the Father, and to the Son, and to the Holy Spirit,
As it was in the beginning, is now, and will be forever. Amen.

Examination of Conscience:

Pray the prayer of the blind man, "Lord, that I might see."
Then close your eyes. Relax and wait. See what comes to mind from your day.
Pray about what comes to mind. – *"Give your cares to God, for God cares for you"*(1
Pet. 5:7). (Or if praying with someone, share your insight/memory and then
begin the rest of night prayer)

Antiphon: In you, my God, my body will rest in hope.

Psalm 16

Preserve me, God, I take refuge in you.
I say to the Lord: "you are my God.
My happiness lies in you alone."

He has put into my heart a marvelous love
For the faithful ones who dwell in his land.
Those who choose other gods increase their sorrows.
Never will I offer their offerings of blood.
Never will I take their name upon my lips.

O Lord, it is you who are my portion and cup;
It is you yourself who are my prize.
The lot marked out for me is my delight:
Welcome indeed the heritage that falls to me!

I will bless the Lord who gives me counsel,
Who even at night directs my heart.
I keep the Lord ever in my sight:
Since he is at my right hand, I shall stand firm.

And so my heart rejoices, my soul is glad;
Even my body shall rest in safety.
For you will not leave my soul among the dead,
Nor let your beloved know decay.

You will show me the path of life,
The fullness of joy in your presence,
At your right hand, happiness for ever.

Glory to the Father, and to the Son, and to the Holy Spirit,
As it was in the beginning, is now, and will be forever. Amen.

Psalm prayer: Lord Jesus, uphold those who hope in you and give us your counsel, so that we may know the joy of your resurrection and deserve to be among the saints at your right hand.

A reading from Paul's first letter to the Thessalonians (5:23)

May the God of peace himself make you perfectly holy and may you entirely, spirit, soul, and body, be preserved blameless for the coming of our Lord Jesus Christ.

Responsory

Into your hands, Lord, I commend my spirit.
  - Into your hands, Lord, I commend my spirit.
You have redeemed us, Lord God of truth.
  - I commend my spirit.
Glory to the Father, to the Son, and to the Holy Spirit
  - Into your hands, Lord, I commend my spirit.

Antiphon: Protect us, Lord, as we stay awake; watch over us as we sleep, that awake, we may keep watch with Christ, and asleep, rest in peace.

Lord, now you let your servant go in peace;
Your word has been fulfilled:
My own eyes have seen the salvation
Which you have prepared in the sight of every people:
A light to reveal you to the nations
And the glory of your people Israel. (Luke 2:29-32)

Glory to the Father, and to the Son, and to the Holy Spirit,
As it was in the beginning, is now, and will be forever. Amen.

Protect us, Lord, as we stay awake; watch over us as we sleep, that awake, we may keep watch with Christ, and asleep, rest in peace.

Prayer:

Lord God,
Send peaceful sleep
To refresh our tired bodies.
May your help always renew us
And keep us strong in your service.
We ask this through Christ our Lord.

Conclusion:

May the all-powerful Lord grant us a restful night and a peaceful death.
- Amen.

Hail Mary

Hail Mary, full of grace,
The Lord is with you!
Blessed are you among women,
And blessed is the fruit of your womb, Jesus.
Holy Mary, Mother of God,
Pray for us sinners,
Now and at the hour of our death.

Friday

Introduction

God, come to my assistance.
Lord, make haste to help me.

Glory to the Father, and to the Son, and to the Holy Spirit,
As it was in the beginning, is now, and will be forever. Amen.

Examination of Conscience:

Pray the prayer of the blind man, "Lord, that I might see."
Then close your eyes. Relax and wait. See what comes to mind from your day.
Pray about what comes to mind. — *"Give your cares to God, for God cares for you"* (1
Pet. 5:7). (Or if praying with someone, share your insight/memory and then
begin the rest of night prayer.)

Antiphon: Day and night I cry to you, my God.

Psalm 88

Lord my God, I call for help by day;
I cry at night before you.
Let my prayer come into your presence.
O turn your ear to my cry,

For my soul is filled with evils;
My life is on the brink of the grave.
I am reckoned as one in the tomb:
I have reached the end of my strength,
Like one alone among the dead;
Like the slain lying in their graves;
Like those you remember no more,
Cut off, as they are, from your hand.

You have laid me in the depths of the tomb,
In places that are dark, in the depths.
Your anger weighs down upon me:
I am drowned beneath your waves.

You have taken away my friends
and made me hateful in their sight.
Imprisoned, I cannot escape;
My eyes are sunken with grief.

I call to you, Lord, all the day long;
To you I stretch out my hands.
Will you work your wonders for the dead?
Will the shades stand and praise you?

Will your love be told in the grave
Or your faithfulness among the dead?
Will your wonders be known in the dark
Or your justice in the land of oblivion?

As for me, Lord, I call to you for help:
In the morning my prayer comes before you.

Lord, why do you reject me?
Why do you hide your face?

Wretched, close to death from my youth,
I have borne your trials: I am numb.
Your fury has swept down upon me;
Your terrors have utterly destroyed me.

They surround me all the day like a flood,
They assail me all together.
Friend and neighbor you have taken away:
My one companion is darkness.

Glory to the Father, and to the Son, and to the Holy Spirit,
As it was in the beginning, is now, and will be forever. Amen.

Psalm prayer: Lord Jesus Christ, you chose to suffer and be overwhelmed by death in order to open the gates of death in triumph. Stay
with us to help us on our pilgrimage; free us from all evil by the power of
your resurrection. In the company of your saints, and constantly remembering your love for us, may we sing of your wonders in our Father's house.

A reading from the prophet Jeremiah (14:9)

Yahweh, you are in our midst,
we are called by your name.
Do not desert us!

Responsory

Into your hands, Lord, I commend my spirit.
    - Into your hands, Lord, I commend my spirit.
You have redeemed us, Lord God of truth.
    - I commend my spirit.
Glory to the Father, to the Son, and to the Holy Spirit
    - Into your hands, Lord, I commend my spirit.

Antiphon: Protect us, Lord, as we stay awake; watch over us as we sleep, that awake, we may keep watch with Christ, and asleep, rest in peace.

Lord, now you let your servant go in peace;
Your word has been fulfilled:
My own eyes have seen the salvation
Which you have prepared in the sight of every people:
A light to reveal you to the nations
And the glory of your people Israel. (Luke 2:29-32)

Glory to the Father, and to the Son, and to the Holy Spirit,
As it was in the beginning, is now, and will be forever. Amen.

Protect us, Lord, as we stay awake; watch over us as we sleep, that awake, we may keep watch with Christ, and asleep, rest in peace.

Prayer:

All powerful God,
Keep us united with your Son
In his death and burial
So that we may rise to new life with him,
Who lives and reigns for ever and ever.

Conclusion:

May the all-powerful Lord grant us a restful night and a peaceful death.
- Amen.

Hail Mary

Hail Mary, full of grace,
The Lord is with you!
Blessed are you among women,
And blessed is the fruit of your womb, Jesus.
Holy Mary, Mother of God,
Pray for us sinners,
Now and at the hour of our death.

Saturday

Introduction

God, come to my assistance.
Lord, make haste to help me.

Glory to the Father, and to the Son, and to the Holy Spirit,
As it was in the beginning, is now, and will be forever. Amen.

Examination of Conscience:

Pray the prayer of the blind man, "Lord, that I might see."
Then close your eyes. Relax and wait. See what comes to mind from your day.
Pray about what comes to mind. — *"Give your cares to God, for God cares for you"*
(1 Pet. 5:7). (Or if praying with someone, share your insight/memory and then
begin the rest of night prayer.)

Antiphon: Have mercy, Lord, and hear my prayer.

Psalm 4

When I call, answer me, O God of justice;
From anguish you released me; have mercy and hear me!

O men, how long will your hearts be closed,
Will you love what is futile and seek what is false?

It is the Lord who grants favors to those whom he loves;
The Lord hears me whenever I call him.

Fear him; do not sin: ponder on your bed and be still.
Make justice your sacrifice and trust in the Lord.

"What can bring us happiness?" many say.
Let the light of your face shine upon us, O Lord.
You have put into my heart a greater joy
Than they have from abundance of corn and new wine.

I will lie down in peace and sleep comes at once
For you alone, Lord, make me dwell in safety.

Glory to the Father, and to the Son, and to the Holy Spirit,
As it was in the beginning, is now, and will be forever. Amen.

Psalm prayer: You consoled your Son in his anguish and released him
from the darkness of the grave. Lord, turn your face toward us that we
may sleep in your peace and rise in your light.

A reading from the Book of Deuteronomy (6:4-7)

Hear, O Israel! The LORD is our God, the LORD alone! Therefore, you
shall love the LORD, your God, with all your heart, and with all your soul,
and with all your strength. Take to heart these words which I enjoin on you
today. Drill them into your children. Speak of them at home and abroad,
whether you are busy or at rest.

Responsory

Into your hands, Lord, I commend my spirit.
- Into your hands, Lord, I commend my spirit.

You have redeemed us, Lord God of truth.
- I commend my spirit.

Glory to the Father, to the Son, and to the Holy Spirit
- Into your hands, Lord, I commend my spirit.

Antiphon: Protect us, Lord, as we stay awake; watch over us as we sleep, that awake, we may keep watch with Christ, and asleep, rest in peace.

Lord, now you let your servant go in peace;
Your word has been fulfilled:
My own eyes have seen the salvation
Which you have prepared in the sight of every people:
A light to reveal you to the nations
And the glory of your people Israel (Luke 2:29-32)

Glory to the Father, and to the Son, and to the Holy Spirit,
As it was in the beginning, is now, and will be forever. Amen.

Protect us, Lord, as we stay awake; watch over us as we sleep, that awake, we may keep watch with Christ, and asleep, rest in peace.

Prayer:

Lord,
We beg you to visit this house
And banish from it
All the deadly power of the enemy.
May your holy angels dwell here
To keep us in peace,
And may your blessing be upon us always.
We ask this through Christ our Lord.

Conclusion:

May the all-powerful Lord grant us a restful night and a peaceful death.
- Amen.

Hail Mary

Hail Mary, full of grace,
The Lord is with you!
Blessed are you among women,
And blessed is the fruit of your womb, Jesus.
Holy Mary, Mother of God,
Pray for us sinners,
Now and at the hour of our death.[31]

---

31 Excerpts from the English translation of *The Liturgy of the Hours* ©1974, International Commission on English in the Liturgy Corporation. All rights reserved.

Appendix II

How Can I Know God's Will For My Life?

"Your will is my heritage forever, the joy of my heart. I set myself to carry out your will in fullness forever" (Ps. 119:111-112).

John English (1924-2004) was a Jesuit priest and writer who was one of North America's pioneers of personal spiritual discernment and guidance. Following is his writing entitled *Discerning Your Vocation*. In our Catholic tradition, there are four possible states of life or vocations we can be called to: single life, married life, priesthood or religious life as a sister or brother. English begins with two examples of people trying to figure out which kind of life God wanted of them:

The first is an example of a person who wished to discover the basic state of life God wished for him. In searching out the dream of God for him he came to a conviction that the Lord wished him to be a priest. So he took this choice to prayer asking the Lord to confirm it. At the beginning there was a sense of peace with the choice. Later, however, there was much disturbance in his inner being: zest for life was disappearing, his mind was concentrated on himself, he experienced sleeplessness, life was becoming a burden and there were other interior experiences. In discussing this with his spiritual director, he indicated that the only way open to someone who wished "to live all perfection" was in the priesthood. When the director suggested to him that it was possible to live the life of perfection in whatever state the Lord called him, he replied quite spontaneously that his deepest desire was to be married and have children. Then he spent some further weeks of further prayer and checking out his inner experience while considering the married state of life. The results were the opposite of those mentioned above: a lightsomeness of being, zest for life, an excitement at new possibilities and a recognition that he could serve other men and women in the married state. He is now a happily married man with three children and much involved in promoting a lay spirituality in everyday life.

We might consider another example almost the opposite of the above. This person fell deeply in love and through much reflection came to the conviction that she was called to the married state. As the time of marriage approached she was much agitated by the thought of her future life. Upon inquiry, it became obvious that these were not just normal fears of a bride to be. In her uncertainty she did not want to hurt the man she loved so much. Still, this question persisted: 'How might I best serve the Lord?' In her being she sensed a great attraction to be present to and serve many persons. Although she did not feel certain that this meant a call to the religious life, it did indicate to her that she needed more confirmation about the married state. A weekend retreat led her to decide to spend some time in a religious order and experience this other state of life. She entered a house of formation and about a year later was surprised to experience the grace of freedom with respect to both states of life. She realized that she could be happy in either state and serve the Lord well in both. She knew that she was free to choose either and that she was to choose the one that most fulfilled her deepest desires. She chose religious life and still feels, after twenty years, that this is her vocation for life.

These two examples indicate that the journey to discovering our life vocation can be twisty indeed. Moreover, they suggest that it is helpful to have a companion or guide with us on our journey.

Vocation comes from the Latin word for call or calling. It implies that there is an action from God who is beyond ourselves beckoning and calling to us. In a sense, we cannot deny this activity. We respond to it by answering yes or no. To ignore it is to answer no. Our belief is that God calls each one of us to do some good in this world. God has a dream for each one of us. We are uniquely loved and called by God. God only wishes good for us as a human race and as individuals. God's dream is that we in our own unique way will join Christ in building a better world and so experience ourselves fully. "*I know the plan I have in mind for you... plans for peace, not disaster, reserving a future full of hope for you... When you seek me you shall find me; when you seek me with all your heart, I will let you find me. It is the Lord who speaks*" (Jer. 29:11-13).

When we wish to discover the basic manner in which we are to live our life, we have a number of ways to proceed depending on the type of persons we are and our life experiences.

Discernment is the activity by which you get in touch with the interior experiences of your being as you consider decisions in the faith...I will now discuss with you in more detail some interior experiences you are to consider as you proceed to discern your vocation:

1. Sense of Identity as the Beloved of God

It is in a context of the love of God for each one of us that we set out to discover our life vocation. For it is in response to God's love for me that I will discover God's desire for me. This love for God flooding my heart draws me to him as I serve other men and women in whatever state of life the Lord calls me to.

2. Overall Goal and Purpose of my Life

Since I am attempting to discover the life vocation that will influence all the other aspects of my life, it is important to reflect deeply on the goal and purpose of all human and Christian life... *"Love one another as I have loved you."* (John 15:12)

3. A Deep Appreciation of the Mind and Heart of Jesus Christ

Since Christians are to put on the mind and heart of Christ in order to fulfill his command, it is important for me to pray over the life of Christ, his words and actions as presented to me in the Gospels. I can do this in many different ways. But a beginning is to read and ponder the accounts given in the New Testament

4. I Pray for Light and Strength

I ask the Lord to move my mind and heart that I may choose the life vocation that will better serve him and his people. I need both clarity and strength. But I also need the strength to overcome the many fears and obstacles that I and others will put in my path.

5. Discerning Interior Movements

As I move through these various steps, many different interior experiences take place in me. Some I have never had before. Some are very strange indeed. Yet, it is good to know that other people before me have had similar experiences when trying to discover their life vocation. Below are some of these experiences, not necessarily in the way you will experience them:

- a sense of being carried, accompanied;
- a sense of sinfulness and unworthiness;
- a great desire to join Christ in building a more just and peaceful world;

- some knowledge of desiring to choose a lesser way and naming it my
vocation; in other words, experiencing deception;
    - some interior experiences that fill me with turmoil and fear;
    - others that fill me with peace and a sense of fulfillment.

6.   Spiritual Counseling

Although this activity is my own since I am the one having the experiences, still a counselor, friend, companion can give me an outside view as I try to discern my life vocation. I seek out someone whom I trust and who has more knowledge of life and of the activities of the Holy Spirit in human beings, a person who can assist me to judge the meaning of my interior experiences.

At some time I may realize that what I need is a few days aside to focus and dialogue with someone more fully on this most important decision of my life. Discernment weekends with other men and women can be a great asset at this time as can a weekend of privately directed prayer at a retreat house. Eventually, I come to a faith-filled certitude that this is what the Lord is calling me to do. I become aware that *"I can do all things in him who strengthens me"* (Phil. 4:13). [32]

---

32 John English, "Discerning Your Vocation." Printed with permission from the Jesuit Vocation Office, 1325 Bay St., Suite 300, Toronto, On. M5R 2C4. **www.jesuits.ca**

Appendix III – The Beatitudes and Saint Marguerite d'Youville

The beatitudes listed in Matthew chapter five sum up what it takes to be a saint, to be beatified. It is good to know the Ten Commandments as a code of morality, but for a Christian, the moral code is summed up in these eight beatitudes. Rather than a list of do's and don'ts, they are a list of qualities a Christian is called to aspire to and nurture. We are responsible not only for what we do, but also for who we become. The beatitudes sum up the kind of person we are called to be as Christians.

Any of the saints we read about were people of great humility who suffered a lot, who followed in Jesus footsteps of the cross and self giving love. One example is St. Marguerite d'Youville, who lived in Montreal, Canada from 1701-1771. She was the Mother Theresa of her time, and is known as the Mother of Universal Charity. All of the saints were people who had a serious commitment to prayer, and allowed the power and joy of God's love to shine through. I once went through a book called *Hands to the Needy*[33] about St. Marguerite d'Youville, to see how she exemplified the beatitudes of Matthew 5:3-10. Here is what I found. I will first give the description of Marguerite d'Youville, followed by the beatitude she exemplifies.

"Marguerite was ingenious in making a little go along way. She never wasted anything: neither words nor acts; neither time nor money; neither the foods that comprised their simple meals nor the hand-woven cloth that made up their garments. She had a sure sense of the fitness of things, and simplicity was its essence." (p. 33)

Happy are the poor in spirit; theirs is the kingdom of heaven.

---

33 Sister Mary Pauline Fitts, *Hands To The Needy*, Yardley, Pennsylvania, The Grey Nuns of the Sacred Heart, 2000.

"Having failed to find the good, the beautiful and the true in the transient treasures of the world, she now sought them in the things of God. She prayed 'Oh, Father of all consolation, be the sole object of our love.'" (p. 65)

Blessed are the pure of heart; they shall see God.

Marguerite's Father died when she was seven. She was a married woman who lived in New France. Four of her six children died in infancy. At the age of twenty-eight, her husband died and left her a widow with children and debt. "Personal suffering had enlarged her heart and had filled it with compassion for the sorrows of others." (p. 77)

Blessed are those who mourn; they shall be comforted.

"Reflective by nature rather than effusive, she spoke little and thought much. To her, deeds, not words, were of prime importance." (p. 30)

Blessed are the gentle; they shall inherit the earth.

Marguerite was the oldest child. "She gave to the younger children an example of respect that fostered harmony and peace." (p. 32) "They were always happy in her company, with a happiness that somehow united them more closely. Never, in the years to come, did Marguerite lose her gift of harmonizing diverse personalities." (p. 33)

Blessed are the peacemakers; they shall be called children of God.

"She was a kind listener who knew how to comfort the sorrowful and counsel the doubtful, to encourage the weak and lift up the fallen." (p. 77) "Searching out the most destitute, the paralyzed, the cripples, the blind, the mentally afflicted, the lonely aged, she would gently bathe their pitiful bodies, wash and mend their clothes, or replace filthy rags with clean whole garments." (p. 83)

Blessed are the merciful; mercy shall be shown to them.

Marguerite ran a store in Montreal. "She was a competent business woman, honest, straightforward, just. Her natural integrity and sense of truth combined with the supernatural virtue of charity to forbid over-charging and every other device of making money beyond the sanctions of equity." (p. 74)

Blessed are those who hunger and thirst for righteousness; they shall be satisfied.

In 1738, Marguerite and three other young women dedicated their lives to God, and the service of the poor in Montreal. People thought that the sisters were continuing her husband's alcohol trade and were getting drunk, or *gris*, as they say in French. As the sisters made their way to church people yelled at them, "*Les soeurs grises!*" or "drunk sisters." The sisters kept their peace and "several men, infuriated by their unassailable peace, picked up stones and savagely hurled them, striking the gentle women as they passed on." (p. 99)

Blessed are those who are persecuted for righteousness sake; the kingdom of God shall be theirs.

Prayer

Prayer of Pope John Paul II at World Youth Day 2002

O Lord Jesus Christ, keep these young people in your love. Let them hear your voice and believe what you say, for you alone have the words of life. Teach them how to profess their faith, bestow their love, and impart their hope to others. Make them convincing witnesses to your Gospel in a world so much in need of your saving grace. Make them the new people of the Beatitudes, that they may be the salt of the earth and the light of the world at the beginning of the Third Christian Millennium! Mary, Mother of the Church, protect and guide these young men and women of the 21st century. Keep us all close to your maternal heart. Amen.

Acknowledgments

I want to thank the many people have led me to faith and prayer. First are my parents, to whom I dedicate this book. I am extremely fortunate to have them as parents. My high school principal at Fr. Henry Carr was also a tremendous influence. Fr. Thomas Mohan, who remains a mentor and inspiration to this day, was a man who gave his all for his students. The power of his witness and care literally saved my life. Fr. Frank Hogan was my pastor in my teen years. His homilies were from the heart and from his experience, and because of that we experienced scripture as *"living and active, sharper than any two-edged sword."* After high school I joined the Christian Brothers and that was where I was introduced to prayer as a discipline and as a way of life. My novice master, Brother Barry Lynch, was an exceptional spiritual director. Barry, your friendship and continued support is very much appreciated.

I am so thankful to my wife, Dorothy, and daughters, Emily and Janet; first of all for their love, but also for their patience with me as I hogged the computer and couldn't stop talking about this project. You are like God, who knows me just as I am and still loves me. Dorothy, Emily and Janet, you mean the world to me.

Thanks to Laura Whelan for her picture of "the sun's light that plays on the trees" used with Day four.

Many people have helped in the writing of this book. Noel Cooper, an accomplished author and long time friend, spent a lot of time editing my original writing when it was very raw. I am very thankful for his help and encouragement. Another good friend, Rick Britton, gave essential feedback. Marina Nemat, bestselling author of *Prisoner of Tehran*, also very generously read my manuscript and was a tremendous help. Michael Hryniuk gave me the benefit of his spiritual insights and support. Deborah Sheldrake also gave many helpful suggestions as well as much appreciated encouragement.

Various staff and students at St. Marguerite d'Youville High School also read my writing and made many helpful suggestions. Lisa Gregori, Andy

Carreiro, and Peter Yan are teachers who edited, while Erica Fresco was tireless in creating the perfect cover with her mother. Students Kim Go, Precious Omoruyi, Stepehen Vani, Nic Baldassarra, Kristina Cumming, Suja James and Natalie Doummar also gave feedback. I am very thankful to our principal, Kevin Greco, for his support, as well as Shelagh Peterson, DPCDSB's head religion consultant. There are many at d'Youville who are a large part of the inspiration for my writing. A community is made of its people, and what a great community it is to be part of!

Made in the USA
Charleston, SC
02 April 2013